CULTURES OF THE WORLD®

ITALY

Jane Kohen Winter/Leslie Jermyn

BENCHMARK BOOKS

MARSHALL CAVENDISH
NEW YORK

PICTURE CREDITS
Cover photo: © H. Armstrong Roberts
AFP: 37, 39, 40, 49, 66, 96 • Art Directors & Trip: 8, 9, 32, 42, 50, 56, 70, 86, 99, 102, 107
• Ellen Barone/Houserstock: 48, 118 • Bes Stock: 4 • Flash: 41 • Focus Team: 11, 14, 26,
43, 47, 73, 126, 130, 131 • Getty Images/Hulton Archive: 19, 22, 24, 25, 77, 100 • Haga
Library: 1, 5, 80, 85, 110, 113, 115, 128 • Dave G. Houser/Houserstock: 6, 44 • Image Bank:
13, 23, 54, 76, 78, 79 • John R. Jones: 88 • Les Voyageurs: 20, 21, 38, 68, 72, 75, 89, 92, 93,
95, 114 • Life File Photographic Library: 10, 34, 36, 57, 63, 82, 97 • Lonely Planet Images:
45, 46, 59, 69 • Marco Polo/Bouillot: 17, 116 • Sheila McKinnon: 16 • Sciacca: 3, 28, 30,
35, 52, 55, 60, 64, 67, 83, 101, 105, 112, 117, 120, 121, 122 • Pietro Scozzari: 65, 125 • Silveira:
90, 94 • Topham Picturepoint: 103

ACKNOWLEDGMENTS
With thanks to Daniela Bleichmar for her expert reading of this manuscript

PRECEDING PAGE
Italian youths in costume for a Carnival celebration

Marshall Cavendish Corporation
99 White Plains Road
Tarrytown, NY 10591
Website: www.marshallcavendish.com

Originated and designed by
Times Books International, an imprint of
Times Media Private Limited, a member of
Times International Publishing

Printed in Malaysia

Library of Congress Cataloging-in-Publication Data
Winter, Jane Kohen, 1959–
    Italy / by Jane Kohen Winter and Leslie Jermyn.—2nd ed.
        p. cm.—(Cultures of the world—2nd edition)
    Summary: Describes the geography, history, government, economy, and culture
of Italy. Includes bibliographical references and index.
    ISBN 0-7614-1500-9
    1. Italy—Juvenile literature. [1. Italy.] I. Jermyn, Leslie. II. Title. III. Series: Cultures
of the world (2nd ed.)
DG417.W56 2002
945—dc21   2002011628

7 6 5 4 3

CONTENTS

The Palazzo Comunale in Bologna, a medieval building remodeled during the Renaissance, is an example of architectural accomplishment in Italy. The bronze statue is of Pope Gregory XIII, a native of Bologna.

A row of gondolas await tourists on the Grand Canal in Venice.

INTRODUCTION

ITALY HAS INFLUENCED PEOPLES far beyond its borders for millennia. Italians have been groundbreakers throughout history: from artists such as Leonardo da Vinci and Michelangelo Buonarroti to composers such as Giuseppe Verdi and Giacomo Puccini to the scientist Galileo Galilei and the explorer Christopher Columbus.

Beautiful Italy is known today for the true quality of its clothes, cars, and cuisine. Milan is a major stop on the international fashion trail. Ferrari and Fiat are among the world's top automakers. Italian pizza and pasta are common daily meals for people in many countries.

Italy was the birthplace of the Renaissance, and its capital, Rome, is the center of the Roman Catholic faith, which is professed by about a billion people around the world.

This book, part of the *Cultures of the World* series, explores what makes Italians unique and how in spirit there is a little Italian in all of us.

GEOGRAPHY

ITALY IS A LONG, THIN PENINSULA that extends from the southern coast of Europe. Its immediate neighbors—France, Switzerland, Austria, and Slovenia—are in the north, where the Alps form a broad arc around the top edge of the country. Four seas water the long coastline of the Italian peninsula and islands.

SOME AREAS AND DISTANCES

Except in the north, Italy is surrounded by water. The country has a coastline of about 4,700 miles (7,560 km), bordered by the Adriatic Sea to the east, the Ionian Sea to the south, the Tyrrhenian Sea to the west, and the Ligurian Sea to the northwest.

Italy has an area of about 116,400 square miles (301,480 square km), which makes it slightly larger than the U.S. state of Arizona. On a map, the Italian peninsula resembles a tall boot extending into the Mediterranean Sea toward the northern coast of Africa, which at its closest point is only about 90 miles (145 km) away. The peninsula is 170 miles (274 km) wide at its broadest point and 708 miles (1,140 km) long.

In addition to the peninsula, Italy also includes a number of islands; the largest two are Sicily and Sardinia. Sicily, with an area of 11,000 square miles (28,490 square km), is separated from mainland Italy by the Strait of Messina, which is less than 2 miles (3.2 km) wide. Sardinia has an area of 9,500 square miles (24,605 square km) and lies 160 miles (257 km) off the Italian coast in the Tyrrhenian Sea. Some of the smaller islands include Elba in the Tuscan Archipelago and Ischia off the coast of Naples.

Italy also has two small independent states within its borders—the Republic of San Marino at just 25 square miles (65 square km) and Vatican City, even smaller at only 0.17 square miles (0.44 square km).

"Italy's silhouette is unique—a high-heeled boot poised to kick Sicily through the straits between Tunisia (northern Africa) and Sardinia. No other country is so immediately recognizable on the map."

—Alessandro Falassi and Raymond Flower in Culture Shock! Italy

MOUNTAINS, LAKES, AND RIVERS

About 35 percent of Italy's landmass has mountains over 2,500 feet (762 m) tall. Flat plains make up less than 25 percent of the land. The two mountain ranges in Italy are the Alps and the Apennines. Italy's tallest mountains are in the Alps. Monte Bianco, the highest peak in Europe at 15,771 feet (4,805 m), lies on the Italian-French border; the Matterhorn, an Alpine peak at 14,692 feet (4,478 m), lies on the Italian-Swiss border.

The Dolomites in the eastern Italian Alps near Slovenia are so named because the terrain consists primarily of dolomite rock, a sedimentary rock found in many parts of the world. The Dolomites are extremely popular with skiers during the winter months.

At the foot of the Alps lie Italy's largest lakes: the 58-square mile (150-square km) Lake Como, the 85-square mile (220-square km) Lake Mag-

Tourists explore on the edges of a crater in Italy.

giore, and the 148-square mile (383-square km) Lake Garda. The western edge of the Alps is the source of Italy's most important river, the Po. The Po valley is the principal plains region, Italy's flattest and most fertile stretch of land.

The Apennines divide Italy in two down its length, extending from the northwest of the country to the southern tip of the peninsula in the province of Calabria and then on to northern Sicily. The highest peak in the Apennines, at just under 10,000 feet (3,047 m), is Monte Corno, northeast of Rome.

NORTHERN ITALY

Italy's northern region consists of the Alps and the Po valley. The mountains shield the Italian Riviera and the lake district from extreme temperatures. Here, tourism is the most important industry. The largest city in the region is Genoa, the center of Italy's shipbuilding industry and the birthplace of Christopher Columbus.

The highest peak in the Dolomites is Monte Marmolada, at 10,965 feet (3,342 m).

The Po valley stretches 280 miles (450 km) from Turin in the west to Udine in the east. The valley contains Italy's most productive farmland, much of which is devoted to growing grain, especially rice, corn, and wheat. The Po valley is also Italy's industrial center.

Venice, on the Adriatic Sea, is another tourist center. Built on 118 islands, this romantic city is noted for its art and architecture. Milan, the capital of Lombardy and Italy's second largest city, is located in the plains region. The country's financial and commercial capital, Milan is Italy's richest city. Turin, the capital of Piedmont, is also an important business center and home to Fabbrica Italiana di Automobili Torino (Fiat).

SOUTHERN ITALY

Southern Italy—consisting of the central and southern regions—is characterized by the rugged terrain of the Apennines. Land in the central region is not as fertile or well-irrigated as in the north. Nevertheless the area is dotted with small farms growing beans, wheat, olives, and the grapes used to produce Chianti wines.

Hotels are built on hillsides at the seaside resort of Sorrento in the south.

The central southern region contains the nation's capital, Rome, and Tuscany's capital, Florence, historically two of the most influential cities in Europe.

Rome has been the capital of modern Italy since 1870. The city's streets and *piazza* ("pe-AHT-zah"), or plazas, are lined with ancient buildings, graceful monuments, and magnificent statues and fountains. Within Rome is Vatican City, probably Italy's most visited site. The Vatican is the center of the Roman Catholic Church and the home of the pope.

Florence rivals Venice in architectural beauty. Florence's charming, winding streets open up into elegant *piazza* filled with churches and their Renaissance treasures.

The most important city in southern Italy is Naples. Crammed with people, cars, factories, and refineries, it is the third largest city in Italy and an important port.

Much of the land in the south is dry and yields little agricultural produce. However, certain areas of Campania have good soil, enriched by volcanic ash that produces excellent fruit and vegetables.

SICILY AND SARDINIA

Sicily is the largest and most beautiful of all Mediterranean islands. Most of its hilly terrain is used to cultivate wheat and beans and as grazing land for sheep. In the shadow of the active volcano Etna (the name is derived from the Greek word *aitho*, meaning "I burn"), tropical fruit trees thrive. The capital of Sicily is the port of Palermo, located on the Tyrrhenian Sea.

Sardinia has few good roads and a harsh, mountainous terrain that is mainly used for rearing sheep and growing wheat, olive trees, and grapevines where irrigation is possible. Sardinia's beautiful beaches are developed for international tourism. The capital of Sardinia is the port of Cagliari on the southern coast.

CLIMATE

Most of Italy enjoys Mediterranean weather, with some climatic variation. While it can get very cold in the Alps in the winter, the peninsula generally experiences milder weather in both winter and summer.

In the plains the short winter can be harsh and the long summer hot. The coastal lowlands are warm even in winter. The highlands in the interior receive a lot of snow.

A hot wind called the *scirocco* ("SHE-roh-koh") blows over southern Italy in the summer, carrying fine sand from the Sahara Desert in northern Africa. Sicily and Sardinia experience long, hot, and dry summers and relatively warm winters.

Whitewashed houses in Sicily protect residents from the hot summer sun.

THE PLANTS OF ITALY

Beech trees, spruce, and other conifers populate the Italian Alps, while the lower altitudes are dominated by oak, chestnut, pine, and poplar. There are also maple, lime, elm, ash, birch, fir, and chestnut trees.

Trees found in the northern lake district include evergreens, cork oak, cypress, and olive. Carob, red juniper, olive, almond, and citrus trees grow in central and southern Italy. The broom that grows around Etna is an endemic species of Sardinia.

ITALY'S ANIMAL LIFE

The Italian Alps are home to deer, wild goats, and a kind of antelope called chamois. Wild bears are found only in the regions of Abruzzi and Trentino-Alto Adige. Wildcats such as the lynx roam the Apennines, and wolves inhabit hills in the south.

Indigenous and migratory birds on the Italian peninsula and on the islands include herons, egrets, bitterns, gulls, terns, swallows, ospreys, harriers, owls, and warblers. Predatory birds include hawks, eagles, and crows. Teals, shovelers, and tufted ducks travel from northern Europe to winter in Italy. Other ducks found in Italy include the great crested grebe, water rail, coot, and moorhen.

The Mediterranean Sea supports a variety of fish such as sardines, anchovies, squid, tuna, swordfish, perch, mullet, sharks, and mackerel. The largest otter population on the Italian peninsula lives at the foot of the Appenines in the Campania region.

Italian reptiles include the marsh tortoise, common toad, salamander, gecko, ululone (a yellow-bellied frog), and the poisonous Orsini's viper. Other regulars in Italy's wildlife scene include hedgehogs, porcupines, badgers, foxes, weasels, hares, wild boar, shrews, field mice, and bats.

EARTHQUAKES AND VOLCANOES

Italy has for centuries been vulnerable to volcanic eruptions and earthquakes. Regions in the Alps and Apennines have had their share of tremors and earthquakes, as have areas around Naples and in the regions of Umbria, Abruzzi, and Friuli-Venezia Giulia in the last 20 years. Among Italy's active

volcanoes are Etna in Sicily and Vesuvius near Naples. One of the country's latest big earthquakes occured in 1997 in Umbria and Marche. It killed 11 people, injured more than 100, and severely damaged the Basilica of St. Francis of Assisi. In 2002 an earthquake of magnitude 5.6 hit Sicily, damaging some buildings, especially in the capital, Palermo.

Probably the most famous eruption in Italy, and one that has fascinated historians for centuries, was the eruption of Mount Vesuvius on August 24 in A.D. 79 that destroyed the Roman cities of Pompeii (*right*) and Herculaneum. The eruption spewed huge amounts of ash and pumice into the sky and within three hours buried the city of Pompeii and the nearby town of Herculaneum under debris, lava, and mud.

Only in the late 19th century did archeologists begin to uncover these ancient Roman cities. Incredibly, they found that the carbon-rich ash had preserved many of the details of daily life in Pompeii. Entire bakeries were found with ovens containing loaves of bread still intact, as well as elegantly painted frescoes on bedroom walls, thousands of scrolls made from papyrus in libraries, statues, seedlings in gardens, and human skeletons. Graffiti on the the walls of buildings could still be read.

In 2001 a team led by archeologist Giuseppe Mastrolorenzo made a startling discovery about how some of the victims of the A.D. 79 eruption had died. Unlike skeletons previously found, the 80 that Mastrolorenzo's team studied, found in boat sheds along the beach at Herculaneum, showed signs that it was not suffocation but intense heat that had killed those victims, vaporizing their flesh in less than a second, before they could even feel the incinerating heat!

Parts of Pompeii still lie buried. While the cost of unearthing and preserving the cities' treasures is exorbitant, resources to finance preservation efforts are scarce.

HISTORY

ALTHOUGH THE ITALIAN REPUBLIC has been in existence for just over 140 years, Italian history goes back to at least one thousand years before the birth of Christ. The history of Italy can be traced over the centuries through the different civilizations and empires that once claimed parts of the land—Etruscans, Greeks, Carthaginians (now Phoenicians), French, Germans, Austrians, Spanish, and the Roman Catholic Church.

Peoples speaking Indo-European languages settled on the Italian peninsula as early as the 16th century B.C. Around 1100 B.C., the Villanovan people came to northern Italy from central Europe, while between 1100 and 700 B.C. the Illyrians migrated from the Balkans to central and southern Italy.

The Etruscans had a strong influence on early Roman society. The first Etruscans arrived in Italy around 1200 B.C. Historians believe that they came from Lydia, an ancient kingdom in present-day Turkey. The Etruscans spoke their own language, now lost, and had a highly developed city culture, with expertise in mining, farming, engineering, road building, sailing, painting, sculpting, and warfare. Etruscan women enjoyed equal status in society. They owned property, kept their names after marriage, and learned to read.

The Etruscans were also respected for their ability to predict the future. They read the entrails, especially the liver, of bulls, goats, and sheep for patterns associated with the signs of the gods.

By about 800 B.C., Greeks and Phoenicians were also present in Italy. They colonized the southern provinces and Sicily, while the Etruscans dominated central Italy, especially the area between the Arno and Tiber rivers. A federation of tribes known as the Latin League flourished in the fertile region of Latium south of the Tiber. Rome was one of the most important states in Latium during the sixth century B.C.

Italy has been ruled by emperors, popes, monarchs, and democratically elected presidents and prime ministers. The country has experienced periods of astonishing development, from the grandeur of the Roman empire and the beauty of the Renaissance to devastating wars and the economic boom of the 1960s.

Opposite: **The Colosseum in Rome was built in the 1st century A.D. at the height of the Roman empire. According to historical records, 50,000 spectators could watch gladiators fight wild beasts or other gladiators.**

THE ROMAN REPUBLIC

The first Roman republic was established in 509 B.C., with Rome as the capital. The city of Rome was built on seven hills: Capitoline, Palatine, Caelian, Esquiline, Aventine, Quirinal, and Viminal. The republic was governed by elected officials instead of monarchs, and the constitution distributed political power by making the leader of the republic answerable to the senate or legislature.

Roman society was divided into three classes. At the top were the members of the aristocracy, the patricians. Next came the plebeians, the common people. At the bottom of the social ladder were the slaves. The male patricians and plebeians could fight in the army and participate in politics, but the slaves were not considered citizens of the republic and had no such rights.

In the early years of the republic, many conflicts arose between the patricians and the plebeians over the latter's involvement in government. The plebeians finally forced the lawmakers to develop a written legal code called the Law of the Twelve Tables. Engraved on bronze tablets, which were displayed in the Roman Forum, this code had great significance for future democracies. It recognized that male patricians and plebeians had equal rights and dealt with such legal matters as writing contracts, property rights, debt, marriage, divorce, and criminal punishment.

EARLY CONQUESTS By 272 B.C. the Romans ruled the whole Italian peninsula, having defeated the Etruscans in the north and the Greeks in the south. In the next century, Rome fought the north African power Carthage for the Mediterranean Sea in the Punic Wars. Finally, in 146 B.C. the Romans destroyed Carthage. Victors in the Punic Wars, they obtained the islands of Sicily, Sardinia, and Corsica, and part of Spain. Victories in the east gave them control of Greece. By 63 B.C. they ruled most of the Mediterranean.

JULIUS CAESAR Julius Caesar further expanded the republic by conquering Gaul (now France). Caesar was a military genius, talented orator, accomplished poet, and historian. Although he was a member of the aristocracy, he supported the plebeian cause. In 45 B.C. Caesar declared himself dictator of the Roman republic and ruler of its vast empire. Caesar believed in equality (he allowed all of Italy's male inhabitants to become Roman citizens), but he also believed that a dictator should have absolute supremacy and be able to choose his successor. Many Roman senators did not agree with him. On March 15 (the Ides of March), 44 B.C., Julius Caesar was stabbed to death by a group of senators, including a man named Brutus, who some believed to be Caesar's illegitimate son.

A statue of Julius Caesar in France reminds the French of the Roman conquest in 49 B.C.

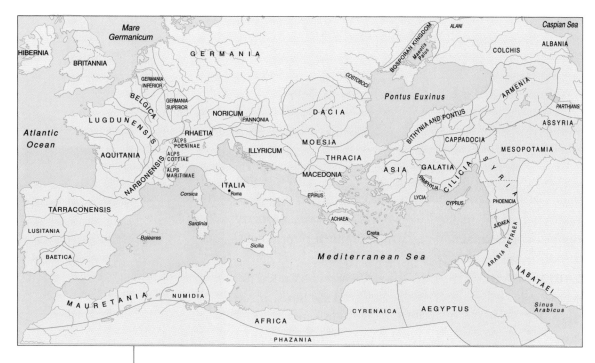

The Roman empire at the end of the second century A.D. extended across most of Europe, northern Africa, and the Middle East.

THE ROMAN EMPIRE

A decade of civil unrest followed Caesar's death, as Julius Octavian, Caesar's nephew, and his fellow triumvir Mark Antony struggled for power. In 31 B.C. Octavian became the first Roman emperor, taking the name Augustus ("the revered").

Emperor Augustus built libraries, temples, theaters, and roads, and established a uniform legal code in the empire. His rule began a time known as Pax Romana, or Roman Peace. The Roman empire reached its peak by the end of the first century A.D., when Roman greatness and the Latin language dominated from the Caspian Sea to the Atlantic Ocean.

By the third century, the empire was in decline. Christianity was widespread, encouraging peace rather than aggression. Roman territories were repeatedly invaded by Asian and Germanic barbarians.

In A.D. 285 Emperor Diocletian divided the empire into the eastern Byzantine empire, ruled from Constantinople (now Istanbul), and the western Roman empire, ruled from Rome. The western empire later fell to the Visigoths and the Vandals from central Europe. The last Roman emperor was deposed in 476, ending the western empire.

LIFE IN THE ROMAN EMPIRE

Life in the Roman empire was filled with pleasures for the wealthy, who lived in large homes with up to 20 rooms, open central skylights, elaborate gardens, and walls decorated with beautiful frescoes. They lounged on couches in the dining room for their meals and visited public bath houses to relax with friends and play dice. Slaves served food and beverages in the bath houses and gave massages to customers and cleaned the baths.

Poorer Romans had small homes and found it hard to get jobs as the slaves did most of the hard work. But they did not starve since all Roman citizens were entitled to free grain. Roman families often went to the temple to make offerings to the gods. Children were taught by Greek slaves at school, and in their spare time they played with small figurines, hoops, balls, and their pet cats and dogs. Boys wrestled and fenced as well.

The Romans fed their love of entertainment by going to the theater. Greek tragedies and comedies, ballet, and mime were popular performances. Audiences were allowed to shout their comments to the actors and dancers on stage.

The Romans also enjoyed watching gladiator fights (*below*), where slaves fought each other or wild animals to the death, and chariot races, where drivers had to stay on their chariots or risk being dragged by the reins or trampled by the horses.

THE MIDDLE AGES

During the next 1,000 years, parts of Italy were attacked and seized by Byzantines, Germans, Arabs, Franks, Normans, French, Spaniards, and Austrians. In A.D. 800, the establishment of the Holy Roman empire brought central Italy officially under the control of Charlemagne (Charles the Great) and the Roman Catholic Church, cutting off the northern region from the south. By the 11th century, the north was controlled by Lombards, a Germanic people with origins in southern Sweden; the central region by the Church; and the south by Normans from northern France.

By the end of the 12th century, much of Italy was divided into small city-states that had achieved some independence from their official rulers. The city-states had strong commercial ties with the rest of Europe and prospered. They were populated by successful merchants and skilled artisans. Many were run by rich and powerful families such as the Visconti of Milan, the Scaligeri of Verona, the Gonzaga of Mantua, and the Medici of Florence.

A Byzantine mosaic in Istanbul shows Byzantine emperors Justinian and Constantine paying tribute to Mary and Jesus. The Byzantine influence in Italy was not only political but cultural and artistic as well. Fine examples of Byzantine-style architecture and mosaics can be found in Rome and Ravenna.

THE RENAISSANCE

In the 15th and 16th centuries, wealthy members of the merchant class contributed to the birth of a great cultural movement in Italy called the Renaissance, or Rebirth. Renaissance thought emphasized the human being as master of his or her destiny rather than as a victim of fate.

The ideal Renaissance person possessed a great deal of knowledge about many subjects, both scientific and artistic. Leonardo da Vinci, for example, was a highly accomplished artist, scientist, and engineer. The Renaissance thinker embraced the classical Greek idea of beauty and art and lived by the ideal that the human being as an individual could direct his or her life in a rational manner.

Cities, the Church, and leading Renaissance families supported the arts, commissioning painters, sculptors, architects, and poets for many projects. Italy thus accumulated a great wealth of art and cultural and philosophical knowledge that had an enormous impact on western European thought and ideas.

The Altar of the Chapel of Princes in Florence, resting place of the Medici family. In 1439 Cosimo de Medici invited classical Greek scholars to an academy he sponsored for the study of Greek philosophy, thereby making Florence a center for the study of the humanities.

FOREIGN DOMINATION

The Italian city-states lost much of their autonomy in the 16th to 18th centuries as the French and Spaniards fought for land in Italy. After the latter half of the 16th century, the Spaniards dominated most of Italy. Only Venice and the duchy of Savoy-Piedmont retained some independence.

Austria became a major power in the north after the War of the Spanish Succession ended in 1713, while the Spanish Bourbons dominated the south and the popes retained their hold over the central states.

At the end of the 18th century, a French republican army led by Napoleon Bonaparte invaded northern and central Italy. By 1799 Napoleon controlled much of Italy and took over its administration. He retrained the Italian army, revised the legal system, built bridges and schools, restored roads, ended the feudal system of land management, and took property away from the papacy. By instituting these reforms and inspiring nationalism among the Italian people, Napoleon gave Italy a sturdy foundation for independence.

Camillo di Cavour.

INDEPENDENCE AND UNIFICATION

After Napoleon was defeated at Waterloo in 1815, the victors restored Italy to its former monarchs: Lombardy and Venetia to the Austrians; the papal states to the pope; and Naples and Sicily to the Bourbons. Piedmont remained an independent Italian state under the rule of the king of Sardinia, Victor Emmanuel I.

In 1831 Giuseppe Mazzini, a revolutionary from Genoa, began the Risorgimento ("ree-sohr-gee-MEN-toh"), or Resurgence, a movement to unify all of Italy. Two other figures played key parts in the Risorgimento movement: King Victor Emmanuel II and his prime minister Camillo di Cavour.

Cavour sought the help of France's Napoleon III after the Piedmontese army fought two losing battles against the Austrians in 1848 and 1849. In the War of Liberation in 1859, Italian and French forces defeated the Austrians and conquered Milan and Lombardy.

In 1860 most of northern and central Italy voted to unite, but the pope did not favor unifying the papal states with the other regions. Giuseppe Garibaldi, a freedom fighter and Mazzini's ally, united southern Italy and the island of Sicily with the north and later took the papal states as well. In March 1861, the United Kingdom of Italy was proclaimed, with Victor Emmanuel II as the first king of its 22 million citizens.

But two territories were still outside the rule of the new kingdom: Venetia (under Austrian rule) and Rome (under papal rule). In 1866 Venetia was ceded to Italy; in 1870 Rome was captured.

THE ITALIAN KINGDOM

Despite having a central government, the new Kingdom of Italy was unstable. Cavour had died soon after unification, and there were no able leaders to take over the job of administering the different regions, each with its own distinct language and customs.

The Victor Emmanuel monument in Rome.

The first 35 years of the kingdom saw 33 governments. The challenges facing the early leaders included widespread illiteracy and poverty. Between 1860 and 1920 millions of Italians emigrated hoping to find a better life elsewhere. The leaders needed to find a way to unify provincial systems of law and taxation and raise national consciousness.

When World War I broke out in 1914, Italy allied itself with Austria and Germany. However, Italy chose not to participate when Austria waged war against Serbia. Italy broke away from Austria and Germany in 1915 and joined forces with the Allies, signing the treaty of London with France, Great Britain, and Russia, in exchange for territory. Italy lost 600,000 men in the war.

Obsessed with his public image, *Il Duce* (as Mussolini called himself) would stand on a stool at official gatherings to look tall and strong.

THE FASCIST ERA

After World War I, Italians turned to Benito Mussolini, a charismatic and ambitious politician, to revitalize the economy and keep communism at bay. In 1921 Mussolini founded the Fascist Party and won 35 seats in the parliament. He was appointed prime minister in 1922 and became dictator in 1925. Mussolini outlawed all political parties except his Fascist Party, dissolved trade unions, censored the press, had his enemies murdered, and created a secret police to deal with opposition.

In 1936 Mussolini conquered Ethiopia. Italy joined forces with Germany, and in 1940 the Axis powers declared war on Great Britain and France. In 1943 the king removed Mussolini from office and signed an armistice with the Allies.

Germany later occupied Italy and reinstated Mussolini in the north, although he had lost nearly every battle in France, Africa, Greece, and Albania. In 1944 Italy realigned against Germany, and in 1945 Italian partisans murdered Mussolini and his mistress.

THE ITALIAN REPUBLIC

In 1946 Italians voted to make Italy a republic. The Christian Democrats won 35 percent of the seats in the new Constituent Assembly.

In 1947 Italy gave up Ethiopia, and a new constitution in 1948 reinstated the freedoms removed by the Fascists and established a parliamentary system. The economy revived in the 1950s, with financial assistance from the United States under the Marshall Plan. In 1957 Italy joined the

European Economic Community and enjoyed great economic growth.

Between 1974 and 1982 terrorist groups tried to bring about social change by murdering politicians (including Christian Democrat prime minister Aldo Moro in 1978), journalists, policemen, or anyone in authority. Many of these terrorists have been sentenced to life in prison.

From 1983 to 1986 Bettino Craxi, the first Socialist prime minister, served the longest uninterrupted term since World War II. In 1992 a corruption scandal implicated politicians from almost all parties. The coalition government led by Giulio Andreotti resigned, and a caretaker government of nonpoliticians led the country to general elections.

In 1994 an alliance of political parties called the Forza Italia won a majority of seats, and Silvio Berlusconi took office as prime minister.

Italy joined the European Monetary Union (EMU) in 1999 and adopted the euro in 2002.

Italian Prime Minister Silvio Berlusconi at the 2001 G8 summit in Genoa.

25

GOVERNMENT

ITALY HAS BEEN a parliamentary republic since June 18, 1946, when Italians voted to abolish the constitutional monarchy that had led the country since 1861 and institute democratic rule. The Italian Republic is governed by the constitution of 1948, which guarantees freedom of speech, thought, and the press.

DIVISIONS OF GOVERNMENT

The Italian government is made up of the president of the republic, a bicameral parliament, a cabinet of ministers, and courts of justice.

The parliament has two chambers: the senate and the chamber of deputies. The senate consists of 315 elected members, former presidents of the republic, and up to five members nominated by the president in office. The chamber of deputies has 630 elected members who represent 32 electoral constituencies. Parliament members serve five-year terms. The two chambers have equal powers, and all laws must be passed by both these bodies.

The president of the republic is the chief of state, elected by the parliament and 58 regional representatives to serve for seven years. He or she has the power to veto laws, but majorities in both parliament houses can override the presidential veto. The executive arm of the government is headed by a president-appointed prime minister, who nominates the members of the cabinet, or Council of Ministers.

The judicial arm consists of civil and criminal courts, administrative courts, and a constitutional court. Italy's judicial system is based on ancient Roman law. Judges dominate in court cases, serving as the "lawyers," who investigate the facts, question witnesses, and decide the verdict, and as the jurors. Juries attend only the most important cases.

LOCAL GOVERNMENT

Italy is divided into 20 regions: 15 with ordinary autonomy, five with special autonomy. The ordinary regions are Abruzzi, Apulia, Basilicata, Calabria, Campania, Emilia-Romagna, Lazio, Liguria, Lombardy, Marche, Molise, Piedmont, Tuscany, Umbria, and Veneto. The special regions are Friuli-Venezia Giulia, Sicily, Sardinia, Valle d'Aosta, and Trentino-Alto Adige.

Each region is governed by a council that can pass laws relating to that region. The council elects the president and members of the executive committee. Italy's special regions are populated by citizens of different cultures, and their councils generally have more freedom than those of the ordinary regions to make legislative decisions.

The immediate concerns of Italian citizens, such as housing, water supply, and garbage collection, are addressed by their communal governments.

The regions are further divided into provinces. Italy has 94 provinces, each governed by an executive council and a governor. The provincial government is responsible for social services and the construction and maintenance of roads among other things.

Italy has more than 8,000 communes—towns, cities, metropolitan centers—run by municipal councils. The communal governments are responsible for urban planning, health, municipal public works, public transportation, and education.

INDEPENDENT STATES

Italy has two independent states within its borders: Vatican City and the Republic of San Marino.

Vatican City, located in Rome, was created in 1929. The Lateran Concordat signed by Cardinal Pietro Gasparri and Benito Mussolini on behalf of Pope Pius XI and King Victor Emmanuel III respectively restored the Catholic Church's political power and exclusive rights to the Vatican since Italy took the papal states in 1870. Vatican City comes under the protection of the Italian police.

The republic of San Marino has an independent government made up of three branches: executive, legislative, and judicial. San Marino has its own constitution and currency and maintains diplomatic relations with other countries.

POLITICAL PARTIES

Italians believe strongly in democracy, and many still fear a takeover by fascists. This is why there are so many parties in parliament. Italian elections are dominated by multiparty alliances such as the House of Liberties (including the Forza Italia and Northern League parties, the Christian Democrats, and the National Alliance) and the Olive Tree Coalition (including the Democrats of the Left, the Daisy and Sunflower alliances, and the Italian Communist Party).

Party power is all-encompassing in Italy. A system of patronage hands out government jobs according to political affiliation. One's job, house, promotion, and pension may depend on the secretary or other official of the local party. If the Christian Democrats run your district, it makes sense to join their party, take part in their social events, and make sure that they stay in power—even if they are incompetent.

Like the U.S. constitution, the Italian constitution of 1948 guarantees certain fundamental rights for each person. It guarantees every citizen personal liberty, freedom of thought and information, freedom of association, and the right to own private property. The constitution also places on every citizen a duty to protect and uphold the laws of the country.

COALITION GOVERNMENTS

The Italian way of government is not as volatile as it may seem. The Christian Democrats have dominated the country's coalition governments since 1945, except between 1983 and 1987, when Bettino Craxi of the Italian Socialist Party was prime minister.

Since 1992, however, when the Clean Hands investigation uncovered a corruption network involving many political parties, the Christian Democrats have split into factions. In the 1994 election, the Socialists won a small number of seats. In 2001 the House of Liberties won the majority in both the senate and chamber of deputies, followed by the Olive Tree Coalition.

Infighting and bickering among so many parties in parliament can make it difficult to settle important issues. The prime minister is sometimes forced to dissolve the cabinet and regroup. On average, Italian governments last only 10 months in office, and Italy has had an average of one government every year since World War II.

ATTITUDES TOWARD GOVERNMENT

The Italian government and civil service are known for being inefficient. Long lines are normal at banks and social service agencies. Applications for government services take years to be reviewed, and government intervention does not often solve problems. Criminal cases can take years to come to trial. Italians rarely pay attention to new laws passed by the government.

A communist rally. Italy's communist party was traditionally the largest in Europe, but in 2001 it won only three seats in the senate and nine in the chamber of deputies.

THE MAFIA—ITALY'S OTHER "GOVERNMENT"

Since the 19th century, the southern regions of Sicily, Calabria, and Campania have been controlled to a large extent by the Mafia. Originally established to maintain order in the lawless regions of Sicily, the Mafia resolved conflicts in the community because there was no effective government. But the Mafia method was often cruel, using intimidation and violent means to achieve results. Members, known as Mafiosi, were sworn to a code of silence that prevented them from testifying against fellow members.

After Italy was unified, the Mafia helped politicians win votes in exchange for favors. Southern Italians looked to the Mafia to protect them and even paid it taxes. Many saw the Mafia as a positive force in the community. Although Mussolini tried to wipe out the Mafia by forcing its members to leave the country, many returned after World War II.

In the late 1970s and early 1980s, the Italian government made a brave decision to halt Mafia activities. Spurred by the murders of anti-Mafia officials and their families, the government made it a crime to be a member of a Mafia organization. In 1987, 14 Mafiosi broke the code of silence to provide incriminating evidence against hundreds of their brothers. Some 338 Mafiosi were convicted in the largest Mafia trial in Italian history.

The murder of two judges in 1992 caused a strong reaction in Italy. In 1993 senior boss Salvatore Riina was arrested; his successor, Leoluca Bagarella, was arrested in 1995. Anti-Mafia efforts continued through the rest of the 1990s, resulting in the arrest of more Mafia bosses. In 2002 some 300 Mafiosi in high-security jails began a hunger strike to protest against the tough conditions of their incarceration—cell isolation, one visit and one phone call a month, and two hours outdoor exercise a day—especially as lawmakers discussed proposals to extend the length of the prison term under such conditions.

The Mafia has inspired books, films, television drama series, and even video games: Mario Puzo's bestselling novel *The Godfather*, adapted by Francis Ford Coppola into the 1972 Oscar-winning movie by the same title; the television series *The Sopranos*, which won four Golden Globes in 2000; and the controversial video game *Mafia: The City of Lost Heaven*.

Somehow, this inefficiency does not seem to bother Italians. Many have either grown to tolerate bureaucratic red tape or have found ways to get around it.

Italians often rely on relatives or close family friends to get things done. Many have little respect for the institution of government. They do not trust government officials, and some do not pay their income taxes.

Even so, Italians do follow political events with a passion. Italian politics is rarely boring.

ECONOMY

THE CONTRAST BETWEEN RICH AND POOR in Italy is stunning. A wealthy northern Italian might shop on Milan's fanciest streets, dressed more fashionably than a wealthy Parisian, while a farm laborer in the underdeveloped south works 10-hour days to make ends meet.

Before World War II, many Italians lived no better than laborers in one of Europe's poorest countries. The post-war years saw the transformation of Italy from a largely agricultural nation to one of the major industrial powers of Europe. This was a period of strong economic and industrial growth now commonly referred to as the Boom.

Between 1945 and 1960 Italy's industrial output expanded by a staggering 150 percent. Industries in the north grew substantially, and many southerners moved north to take up factory jobs. Advanced farm machinery replaced human labor and changed the country's economy from a primarily agricultural one to an industrial one. Income levels doubled, and people began saving and investing their money.

By the 1960s unemployment in Italy was almost negligible. By the 1970s Italy ranked among the world's top seven industrial powers. As economic growth continued into the 1980s, at a slower but still reasonable rate of 3 percent per year, Italy displaced Britain as the fifth largest industrial power in the world, following the United States, Japan, Germany, and France.

The Italian economy slowed in the 1990s to an average annual growth rate of 1 to 2 percent growth annually, before picking up again in the new millennium, with a more than 2.5 percent annual growth rate.

Italians are Europe's biggest savers, saving an average of 21 percent of their income. With their industrial and economic talents, Italians have been called Europe's most adaptable and innovative entrepreneurs.

Opposite: **Shoppers in the Galleria Vittorio Emanuele in Milan.**

TRADE AND EMPLOYMENT

Italy's primary natural resources include natural gas and crude oil, fish, coal, and land for farming. The country trades internationally in minerals and metals, textiles and clothing, vehicles, and food products.

The port of Brindisi in the south. Italy's exports consist largely of manufactured goods.

Italy's main trading partners are Germany, France, the Netherlands, Spain, and the United States. About 10 percent of Italian exports go to the United States, and 5 percent of Italy's imports come from the United States. But the bulk of Italy's trade occurs within the European Union (EU), of which Italy is a member. About 60 percent of Italy's imports come from EU countries, which buy about 57 percent of Italian exports.

Most of the 23.4 million working Italians are employed in one of three sectors: agricultural, industrial, or service. The service sector employs 62 percent of the labor force, industry 32 percent, and agricultural production 5.5 percent.

Italy's unemployment rate was 10.4 percent in 2000. The Italian definition of unemployment includes not just first-time job seekers and people between jobs, but also housewives and students seeking paid employment. Stimulating industry and employment, especially in the agricultural south where an average of 20 percent of the labor force are jobless, is a central concern of the government.

AGRICULTURE

Italy's agricultural products include wheat, corn, soybeans, tomatoes, potatoes, sugar beets, citrus fruit, grapes, and olives. Italy is the world's largest producer of wine and olive oil. Olives are grown mainly in the southern regions of Apulia and Calabria, while wine is produced in every region. Although Italy cultivates a large amount of wheat, it still imports substantial amounts, mostly from its EU trading partners.

Farms occupy about 25 percent of Italy's total land area. Most farms are small—about 7 acres (3 hectares)—and family owned. Only 5.5 percent of the labor force are employed in agriculture today, compared to more than 50 percent before World War II.

Agriculture is still an important part of the industrialized Italian economy.

MINING AND ENERGY

Italy is one of Europe's poorest countries in mineral resources. It has natural reserves of iron ore, feldspar, quartz, sulfur, coal, mercury, and zinc, but imports other minerals.

Most of Italy's natural gas supply is imported; the rest is produced in the Po river valley. The government is working to reduce the nation's use of crude oil in favor of coal and natural gas.

A 1987 referendum rejected the use of nuclear power in Italy, and construction of nuclear power plants was abandoned. But Italy may have to rethink its nonnuclear policy in order to meet its energy needs; more than 75 percent of its energy is imported.

INDUSTRY

Italy's heavy industry is concentrated in the Milan-Turin-Genoa triangle in the north. Major industrial products include steel, iron, computers, motor vehicles, chemicals, and textiles. Italy also has a large petroleum refining industry.

Italian industry is driven by a few large corporations and many small and medium-sized enterprises. Three top Italian companies are Olivetti (computers), Fiat (automobiles), and Pirelli (tires). Small enterprises are considered the backbone of Italy's economy. The country has more small family establishments than do other European countries. Italians like to keep their businesses small so that the family can maintain control.

Businesses in the same industry tend to gather in one location. For example, Italian silk manufacturers are located in Como and ceramic makers in Sassulo.

FASHION Italian fashion has brought great distinction to the country. Italian designers are known for their bold and innovative experiments with color and form.

Milan is the fashion capital of Italy. The city is home to some of the world's most important design labels: trendy clothing for young people by Luciano Benetton; exquisite men's and women's wear by Giorgio Armani; Krizia knits by Mariuccia Mandelli; elegant clothing in unusual fabrics by Miuccia Prada; Missoni sweaters by Ottavio and Rosita; Gucci "classic" clothing and accessories; and shoes by Ferragamo, the company that preserves founder Salvatore's "art of the shoe." Every October, fashion editors and buyers from around the world gather in Milan to view the season's collections.

One of Italy's most important fashion designers was Gianni Versace. Born in 1946 in Calabria, he moved to Milan in 1972 and was part of the first wave of designers who put the city on the fashion map. In 1989 he began to design haute couture, or high fashion, and soon became famous for his innovations in women's wear. With his sister and brother-in-law, he created a multimillion-dollar empire. In 1997 he was shot outside his home in Miami. His family continues to run the Versace fashion empire.

Italian fashion sets the trends for international designers.

SERVICES

About 62 percent of the labor force is employed in the service sector, including tourism, an important sector of the economy, with 40 million tourist arrivals every year.

THE ITALIAN WORK DAY

Italians maintain a healthy balance between work and leisure. Work is often a family affair, and a lot of time off is also spent with the family. Italians generally do not spend as much time at work as many North Americans do. Shops in Italy usually close for a few hours in the middle of the day and stay open into the evening. Only restaurants stay open in the middle of the day.

These are the work hours in general: most businesses in the north operate from 9 A.M. to 5 P.M., with a one-hour lunch break. In the central and southern regions, businesses operate from 9 A.M. to 1 P.M. and 3 P.M. to 7 P.M. Banks and government offices are usually open only from 8:30 A.M. to 1:30 P.M.

Italians generally work five-day, 40-hour weeks. They have 10 paid holidays and six weeks of paid vacation. Many receive a bonus of one month's salary in December and a cost-of-living increase every quarter. Employers may sometimes help pay for employees' transportation and housing costs, with some even contributing toward school fees for employees' children.

FOCUS ON FIAT

Founded in 1899 in Turin, Fiat (named from the acronym for Fabbrica Italiana di Automobili Torino) is Italy's largest and most famous automobile manufacturer. The corporation specializes particularly in cars with low energy-consumption but also makes other vehicles such as trucks and aircraft and delivers other kinds of products and services such as insurance and agricultural and construction machinery.

Fiat is Italy's largest company and the world's sixth largest automobile manufacturer, operating in 61 countries and earning more than US$56 billion a year.

The corporation's automobile sector produces cars under the Fiat, Ferrari (*below*), Lancia, Maserati, and Alfa Romeo lines and sells some 2.5 million vehicles a year.

Fiat cars, especially Alfa Romeos, have won races and awards across Europe. Fiat is one of Europe's most recognized export brandnames, and its buses and tractors can be found across the continent.

In 2000 the automobile sectors of Fiat and the world's largest car maker, U.S.-based General Motors, entered an agreement to merge aspects of ownership and production.

ECONOMIC PROBLEMS

Italy's two main economic problems since its impressive post-war record are its large budget deficit and wide income disparities.

Italy's budget deficit is due in large part to widespread tax evasion. Many Italians from different walks of life—professionals, small business people, laborers, even the rich and famous—do not pay taxes on additional income. Experts estimate that if people's earnings in this submerged economy were accounted for, Italy's gross domestic product (GDP) figure would be about 20 percent greater.

The budget deficit was a major barrier to Italy's entry to the European Monetary Union (EMU), which regulated currency and economic policy. At 6.5 percent in 1996, the deficit was far greater than the 3 percent maximum to qualify for membership. Italy underwent political and

A store employee puts up a sign welcoming the new euro currency in Italy.

economic reform to get into shape. The government sold public industries and cut wage protection and social security to try to balance the budget.

When the euro was launched in 1999, Italy's budget deficit had fallen to 2 percent, less than the 3 percent requirement. Although the country failed to meet another EMU entry criterion (its national debt exceeded 60 percent of the GDP), Italy still made it into the club of nations sharing the euro. In 2002 Italy sustained a budget deficit of 1 percent of the GDP.

A southern Italian lays figs in the sun to dry.

Wide wealth gaps exist between the economically disadvantaged south—which has been compared to a third-world or underdeveloped country—and the industrialized north. The poorest regions in Italy are Calabria and Campania. The south records a high unemployment rate of 20 percent, a situation compounded by higher illiteracy and birth rates than in the north.

As a result, income levels are considerably lower in the south. The per capita income in Palermo in Sicily is only half that of Turin in the northern region of Piedmont. Industrial development in the south is also far behind that in the progressive north. Although the government offers incentives to industries to relocate in the south, many major corporations hesitate to do so because of Mafia activity in much of the region. The economy in the south has thus remained largely agricultural and pastoral.

ENVIRONMENT

ENVIRONMENTAL PROTECTION IN ITALY was practiced as far back as ancient Roman times. The scholar known as Pliny the Elder (A.D. 23–79), in his 37-volume study of life titled *Natural History*, described how the Romans managed their natural resources, with systems for administering forests, for classifying protected forests, and even for tree-planting.

The first wildlife reserves were set up in the 19th century as hunting areas for royalty, and the first national park was set aside in 1922.

Today, faced with the challenge of developing industry to create employment opportunities, Italians have returned to their heritage of environmental consciousness. Membership in regional and international government organizations such as the European Union (EU) is also a strong motivation for Italy to preserve its natural environment.

Left: **A peculiar landmark—the mushroom-shaped tufa rock on the island of Ischia in the Gulf of Naples.**

Opposite: **A breathtaking bayview in Sardinia.**

Graceful cypress trees on the hills of Tuscany.

PROTECTING NATURE'S GIFTS

Blessed with fertile volcanic soil, Italians have enjoyed the fruits of the earth for centuries. Over time, however, human settlement has greatly altered much of the country's natural landscape. Due to systematic logging in the 19th century, only 23 percent of the country is now forested, while crops and pastures occupy 25 percent of the land. Denuded mountain slopes suffer from erosion and landslides.

Italians have been making efforts to protect what remains of their country's virgin forests since the early 20th century, and in 1988 the government formulated the first comprehensive forestry policy. One key proposal is to convert abandoned farmland to forest.

The main threats to Italy's wildlife are habitat loss and sport hunting, which have wiped out a significant proportion of the original wildlife, leaving the surviving species in protected areas. Italy has few large mammals: small populations of wolves, bears, and lynx in remote mountain areas and larger numbers of ibex, chamois, and red deer in the national parks. Hawks are common, but eagles are a rare sight.

Pollution in the Mediterranean Sea is a threat to Italy's marine life, including the monk seal, fin whale, and dogfish shark, which are now threatened or endangered species. Human activity on beaches, where turtles lay their eggs, reduces these gentle reptiles' chances of survival.

Italy has taken measures to clean up its inland waterways and help reduce the human impact on the Mediterranean Sea. The country's five national parks and other national and regional reserves and protected areas are refuges for surviving flora and fauna.

Mountain sheep graze in the natural park at the upper Pesio and Tanaro valleys in Piedmont.

ABRUZZO AND THE LYNX

The Abruzzo National Park (*below*), near the town of Pescasseroli, just a two-hour drive from Rome, was established in 1923. The main section of the park covers about 155 square miles (401 square km), but there are reserves surrounding it that bring the total protected area of Abruzzo to about 235 square miles (609 square km). Hardwood forests cover two-thirds of this area; beech, oak, ash, maple, and wild oak are found here. Some of the animals that live in the Abruzzo National Park are Marsican brown bears, chamois, mountain goats, foxes, and Apennine wolves. Many of these animals have been hunted to extinction outside the park.

In 1972 a cryptozoologist (a scientist who specializes in finding rare and endangered animals), Franco Tassi, shocked the biological community in Italy by suggesting that the Abruzzo National Park might still contain the lynx, a wildcat with short legs and a short tail. The lynx was long believed to have disappeared from the Italian landscape in ancient times. As manager of Abruzzo, Tassi and his team began to look for evidence of the lynx's existence. In 1995 they did a census, estimating that there were some eight to 10 lynxes in the park, and the same year two pairs of lynxes mated.

This was a happy story for Italy's wildlife; it is not often that animals once thought to be extinct are rediscovered in their natural habitat. Tassi thinks that the lynx may be on the rebound in the central and southern Apennines.

FIGHTING AIR POLLUTION

Italy's biggest environmental problem is air pollution. The country ranks among the top five in the world with the highest number of cars owned per person. Fumes from factories and vehicles damage historic buildings and harm people's health. In 2002, when a two-month dry spell triggered a smog emergency in Milan (which lies under a chronic smog cloud in the Po valley) and other cities in the northern Lombardy region, authorities advised people to avoid jogging or taking their babies out in strollers.

Italy passed a Clean Air Act in 1966. In an attempt to reduce industrial carbon emissions, Italy has turned to natural gas, a cleaner fuel alternative than coal. Italy set up its environment ministry in 1986 and, in the 1990s, began to implement policy changes in line with its obligations as an EU member state.

The sleek Pendolino electric train built by Fiat tilts at curves to travel faster even on winding tracks. Today the Pendolino also runs in Spain, Germany, Finland, Switzerland, and Portugal.

EU member states are bound by the Kyoto Protocol, which represents the world's response to the thinning of the ozone layer caused by carbon gases. At the 1997 meeting in Kyoto, Japan, involving 160 countries, developed nations agreed to reduce their carbon emissions by 8 percent from 1990 levels by around 2010. Italy's antipollution measures, such as taxing oil more heavily than natural gas and installing electric-powered modes of transportation, are part of its efforts to fulfill its environmental responsibilities within the EU and the global community.

The government and "green" organizations are not the only ones involved in the fight against pollution. The Fiat corporation has shown how corporations can do their part; Fiat has signed an agreement to reduce emissions from its vehicles by 23 percent by 2010.

CREATIVE SOLUTIONS

Italians have come up with some wonderful ideas for reducing their dependence on conventional, environmentally unfriendly technologies such as gas-powered cars and coal-fired energy plants.

CAR-SHARING In 1999 Italy pilot-tested an electric car-sharing program in nine major cities including Milan, Rome, Turin, Florence, and Bologna. Each city received some 500 to 600 cars, which were made available in parking areas around the city for members of the program to use. People joined the program by paying a membership fee of US$80 to US$300. They then received a special card with which to start an electric car and paid according to how far they traveled.

The smart car, perfect for Italy's narrow streets, also comes in an electric-powered version.

CAR-FREE DAY In February 2000, 174 Italian cities participated in the nation's first "no-car Sunday." To encourage car owners to leave their vehicles at home that day, public transportation was made free in many cities. Museums also waived their entrance fees to encourage people to spend the day enjoying the exhibits.

Italy's car-free day has since been repeated every first Sunday of the month from February to May every year. Pollution levels in Turin have fallen by as much as 56 percent on "no-car Sunday." Going car-free in the long run, however, means more than leaving the car at home for a few hours one day of the month; it means a lifestyle change, a committed decision on the part of car owners to give up their cars and switch to bicycles or rented cars.

SOLAR POWER The 10,000 Photovoltaic Roofs program is the Italian government's five-year plan to equip 10,000 buildings nationwide with rooftop solar panels for electricity generation by 2003.

ITALIANS

WITH A POPULATION of more than 57.5 million, Italy is one of the most crowded nations in Europe. The average nationwide population density is 507 inhabitants per square mile (196 per square km). However, the distribution is uneven. Most Italians live in large cities and on the coasts and plains. Campania, Lombardy, and Lazio are the most densely populated regions, each with more than 777 inhabitants per square mile (300 per square km). Many other areas are still underpopulated. Valle d'Aosta, Basilicata, and Sardinia are the least densely populated regions, with fewer than 181 people per square mile (70 per square km) each.

Urban Italians account for about two-thirds of the population. Rural Italians made up about half the population before World War II, but they have increasingly moved to the urban areas. Rome is the most populous city, with more than 2.7 million inhabitants. Milan, Naples, and Turin follow, with around 1 million inhabitants each. Palermo and Genoa are home to between 650,000 and 700,000 people each, Bologna and Florence to around 400,000 each.

Despite being predominantly Roman Catholic, Italy has one of the lowest fertility rates in the world. Women living in the northern regions tend to have fewer children than the 1.18 national average, while women in the southern regions tend to have more. The infant mortality rate in the north is also lower than in the south.

With approximately nine births, 10 deaths, and 1.7 migrants to every 1,000 of the population, Italy is rapidly reaching zero population growth. Experts believe that the population could fall below 56 million by 2010. A longer average lifespan due to improved health care and a low rate of population growth have resulted in an aging society. More than 18 percent of Italians are 65 years old or older, compared to approximately 14 percent under age 15.

"And don't, let me beg you, go with that awful tourist idea that Italy's only a museum of antiquities and art. Love and understand the Italians, for the people are more marvellous than the land."

—*E.M. Forster*

Opposite: **A Sardinian in traditional dress.**

ETHNIC GROUPS

An ethnic German wearing *lederhosen*, traditional German-Austrian attire, in the northernmost region of Trentino-Alto Adige. This region was part of Austria's Tirol province until World War I. German-Italians account for 0.25 percent of Italy's population.

Italians in the north differ from their southern counterparts not just in lifestyle and wealth, but also in physical appearance. Northern Italians generally look similar to German and French people, whose ancestors conquered northern Italy in past centuries. In contrast, southern Italians, taking after their ancient Greek colonizers, have a distinctly Mediterranean look, with a darker skin tone, dark hair, and brown eyes.

Several minority groups live in Italy's different regions: French-speakers in the Valle d'Aosta region along the French and Swiss borders; German-speakers around the city of Bolzano in the Trentino-Alto Adige region along the Austrian and Swiss borders; Slovene-speakers in Friuli-Venezia Giulia; and Albanians in small communities in the southern regions.

Immigrants from Ethiopia, Egypt, and the Philippines also live and work in Italian cities such as Rome. They generally congregate in certain sectors of the city and establish their own neighborhoods and shops. The bigger cities also attract gypsy families, mostly from eastern Europe, but their numbers are difficult to calculate. The immigrant population in Italy is estimated at over 1 million.

MIGRATION

One factor that has profoundly affected Italy's population patterns is migration, both within and across the country's borders. Since the mid-1800s, millions of Italians have resettled in other parts of the world. Between 1850 and 1880, more than 100,000 Italians left the country annually, many from the south. They headed first for France and Switzerland and later for North and South America.

By 1910 more than 6 million Italians had settled in the United States. The U.S. Immigration Department then implemented a literacy test for immigrants. In 1921 a quota system was imposed, limiting the number of Europeans migrating to the United States. In 1924 the newly enacted National Origins Act further restricted entry into the United States, especially for immigrants from southern and eastern Europe.

Italian emigration picked up again after World War II. Between 1946 and 1973, 8 million Italians left their country and settled in Germany, France, and Switzerland.

Not until 1973 did Italy's massive international migration patterns reverse, as more Italians returned home and fewer left the country. Emigration continued to ease in the 1980s, and immigration intensified. Today Italy has a net international migration rate—the difference between the number of immigrants and emigrants in proportion to the population—of 1.73 migrants for every 1,000 population. In 1999 at least 50 percent of Italy's immigrants came from Albania, China, Morocco, Romania, and the Federal Republic of Yugoslavia.

Internal migration often takes the form of rural-urban migration. In the 1950s and 1960s, many Italians moved from the south and northeast to Rome and the growing Milan-Turin-Genoa industrial area in search of employment and a better quality of life.

"In the heart of every man, wherever he is born, whatever his education and tastes, there is one small corner which is Italian, that part which finds regimentation irksome, the dangers of war frightening, strict morality stifling, that part which loves frivolous and entertaining art, admires larger-than-life-size solitary heroes, and dreams of an impossible liberation from the strictures of a tidy existence."

—from *The Italians* by Luigi Barzini

A Sardinian. Many prosperous and progressive northerners look down on their poorer southern compatriots.

REGIONALISM

Many Italians identify more strongly with their region than with their nation. It is not unusual to meet Italians who insist that they are Tuscan or Venetian or Piedmontese, not just Italian.

People from different regions and cities are associated with certain personality traits. For example, Piedmontese are perceived to be prouder and more reserved than people from other regions; Milanese are said to be more business-minded and sophisticated; Neapolitans are known to be easygoing; Romans are perceived to be aggressive and Venetians passive; and Florentines love to try new things but continue to revere their Renaissance past.

If there is any animosity among Italians from different parts of the country, it is strongest between urban north and rural south. The south, below the imaginary Ancona Wall stretching from the Adriatic port of Ancona to southern Rome, is also referred to as the *Mezzogiorno* ("med-zoh-JOR-noh"), which means "Land of the Midday Sun." The south occupies about 40 percent of Italian land and is home to around 33 percent of the population, but contributes only 20 percent of the GDP.

Many northerners, particularly those living in the country's most important industrial cities regard the primarily agricultural and pastoral south as being backward. Since World War II, the Italian government has spent billions of dollars to raise the standard of living in the south, but the economic and social gap between the two regions continues to widen. Northern Italians resent the government's focus on the south and what they consider a misuse of taxpayers' money. They feel that the money goes straight into the corrupt hands of the Mafia, whose influence is still strong in the south. Southern Italians, on the other hand, feel that the north has long meddled in their affairs without making much progress.

A blue-collar worker. Social status used to be determined by wealth, family history, and family connections. Today it is increasingly being measured by merit and education.

CLASS DISTINCTIONS

While Italy does have a class system, there is more mobility between classes than in other western European nations. Some social scientists divide Italy's social system into the elite or governing class, the middle class, the urban proletariat, and the rural class. The elite class (about 10 percent of the population) is made up of the nation's intellectuals and professionals and also wealthy business people and landowners. The middle class (about 35 percent of the population) is made up of people with some education and defined job skills, such as white-collar workers, artisans, and small businessmen. The urban proletariat (about 35 percent of the population) consists of the less educated but stable working class. The rural class (about 20 percent of the population) consists of small landowners, tenants of landowners, and day laborers. Some hold additional part-time jobs, while others are migrant farmers who travel from region to region, finding work where they can.

LIFESTYLE

ONE THING VISITORS to Italy notice right away is the people's openness and sociable nature. Whether they live in a *palazzo* ("pah-laht-zoh") or a small apartment, Italians have a love of life and enjoy life's pleasures to the fullest.

Looking good is important, and many Italians have a natural flair for style. Italians are also known for their love of art, and they encourage creativity in their children.

A few seeming contradictions mark Italian culture. Although Italians admire cosmopolitanism, for example, they also respect tradition. They dislike authority yet accept government inefficiency with little complaint. Italians are highly individualistic, but they respect the institution of the family and generally make dutiful sons and daughters and responsible mothers and fathers.

Unlike in many North American cities where commercial activities are segregated from residential areas, in Italy shops, offices, houses, and apartments mingle together seamlessly. Downtown areas are still alive and bustling in the evenings, when shops and offices have closed. Most buildings have storefronts facing the street and apartments facing the interior courtyard.

Almost every block has restaurants and cafés, so the streets maintain a buzzing social atmosphere nearly every hour of the day and night.

Above: **Apartment living is a way of life in the city.**

Opposite: **Milanese cycle past old buildings.**

57

APARTMENT LIVING

Most Italians live in cities, where multistory apartments are the dominant form of housing since they make the best use of limited urban space. A typical modern apartment occupies around 1,000 square feet (93 square m). Large cities such as Milan, Rome, and Naples face the problem of providing adequate, affordable housing for the lower and middle classes. The poor often live in small, two-room dwellings or in shanties on the outskirts of the city. In Rome, rents are high, and new apartments come without closets, light fixtures, and kitchen appliances. In older buildings plumbing can be unreliable and elevators may not always work or users may have to insert a coin before the door opens. Electricity is expensive, so central heating is only used when necessary.

VILLAS

Italian villas, or country houses, are usually made of brick or stone, with a tiled roof, and have two levels and an enclosed courtyard. Villas built in the 17th century can still be seen in the rural and suburban areas. They have two or more levels, several courtyards, and elaborate columns.

A group of 16th-century villas near Venice attracts art historians and tourists every year. The villas, including the Villa Trissino and Villa Capra, were the work of Andrea Palladio (1508–80), the most influential Italian Renaissance architect. Palladio invented a new style of housing—the country house—to meet both the practical and aesthetic needs of noble families living in the countryside. The Palladian style later spread to northern European countries such as England.

Old villas in Italy's big cities may look a little rundown on the outside but are often magnificent on the inside, with windows framing views of quiet and peaceful courtyards. Many old villas have been restored and redecorated, with marble floors, high ceilings, and antiques or modern Italian-designed furniture. These serve as holiday homes for the wealthy or "inns" for tourists. The larger villas may have a swimming pool in the courtyard and house five or more apartments.

Many upper-class Italian families own villas in the countryside where they go to spend their weekends or holidays. Some of these estates have been passed down for generations; others are old farmhouses that have been renovated for modern living. In the countryside, the lower floor of the villa may be used to store farm equipment; in the city, it may function as a shop, garage, or office. The family usually lives on the second floor, while guest bedrooms fill the higher floors.

Villa Pignatelli sits in a park, with a Neapolitan city view behind.

NATURAL ELEGANCE

Italians are very conscious of their physical appearance and the image that they project to others. Projecting an image of refinement and culture known as *la bella figura* ("lah BEL-lah fe-GOO-rah") is important to Italians of all social classes, from both the cosmopolitan north and the underdeveloped south. Italians show *la bella figura* in many ways: they behave considerately; they bring flowers or gifts to thank their host for dinner; they give and receive favors and compliments gracefully.

Urban Italians dress well for work. They wear stylish Italian-made clothes to the office: an exquisitely cut suit with a silk tie for men; a soft skirt and blouse and fine leather heels for women.

Italians almost never wear shorts when going to a large city. They wear jeans, but their casual attire is often of high quality. When going to the opera, men wear suits and ties and women wear evening dresses. Black-tie attire is appropriate for opening nights at the famous opera houses.

Italians love wine, but they rarely drink themselves drunk, as this would make them appear slovenly and out of control.

La bella figura shows even in towns and villages, especially on major feast days when visitors join the festivities.

Well-dressed promenaders in San Remo.

INSTITUTIONAL INEFFICIENCY

Although Italians pay attention to individual competence, they have had to put up with incompetence on the part of institutions and bureaucracies. The postal service, transportation system, telephone company, hospitals, schools, and government offices are notorious for being inefficiently managed and chaotic.

Domestic mail takes at least seven days to reach the addressee. Local checks take six days to clear, foreign ones take 15 days. Trains and buses rarely run on time, and the major cities have appalling traffic jams and pollution problems.

The telephone system is confusing, with four-, five-, six-, seven-, and eight-digit phone numbers. Only half of all calls get through with the first dial. Installing a new phone can take up to a year. The use of cellphones seems to have solved some problems, but they have become so popular that people use them even in church!

Despite an increase in the number of state and private hospitals, especially in the central and southern regions, the health care system still faces the problems of rising costs and bureaucracy. Schools follow rigid administrative rules, and staff at government offices face stacks of unprocessed forms.

Even the legal system is affected. Italy is said to be the land of 250,000 laws. Acts passed in ancient times are still in use today, along with the modern legislation. Laws are often modified several times before reaching the statute book.

Most Italians have grown accustomed to institutional inefficiency in their country. They pay more attention to personal relationships instead and are governed by social institutions such as family and the Church. Government rules and regulations are not nearly as effective in keeping chaos at bay as is a son's duty to his mother or a sinner's to God.

Italians appear to be resigned to the fact that their country does not run as smoothly as some other European nations do.

POLITICAL PATRONAGE

One reason why Italy's public services do not operate efficiently is a deep-rooted system of political patronage. Civil servants are recruited based on who—not what—they know. They are also employed for life and therefore have no fears about getting fired.

Many government employees in Italy get their jobs because they belong to the same political party as the person who handles the recruitment. So if the head of a department is a member of the Christian Democrats, for instance, he will hire a Christian Democrat applicant in exchange for a vote for the party in the next election. The new recruit might not believe in the political stance of the party's election candidate, but will vote for him or her anyway in return for the favor that must be repaid.

The civil service and political system have suffered as a result of this system, because a bureaucrat or elected official may not always be the best person for the job or even competent. Political patronage is widely practiced in Italy, a country with over 2 million civil servants, most of them southerners. Between 1973 and 1990, 350,000 Italians were recruited to the civil service through patronage, compared to 250,000 based on merit.

Jobs in Italy's civil service may be secure, but they do not necessarily pay well. Many government employees hold a second and even a third job to supplement their main source of income. Some civil servants sell products to other civil servants while on the job or manage their own business during office hours. Some others even leave the office after lunch to report to their second job, without being reprimanded.

IMPORTANCE OF THE FAMILY

Italians may not be wholeheartedly loyal to government or nation, but they are truly devoted to family. The individual matters a lot, but not at the expense of the family. Italians believe that the family name is all-important and should not be tarnished by the thoughtless acts of one family member. Pride in the family and the desire to keep family ties and values strong have probably been responsible for keeping the country together and enabling it to prosper in spite of its economic, social, and political problems.

Italians spend more time together as a family than do people from many other Western cultures. The traditional Italian family is based on the patriarchal institution—it is headed by the grandfather, who passes his authority on to the eldest son, who does the same to his first son, and so on through the generations. Children usually live with their parents until they get married. Then they join the family business, set up house near their parents, eat with them, visit them, and travel with them. More aged parents live with their children in Italy than in the United States, and many Italians feel that it is their duty to care for their parents themselves rather than place them in a nursing home. The grandparents help make important domestic decisions and often take care of the children when the parents go to work.

In the northern, highly industrialized areas of Italy, the influence of the traditional family has dwindled as society has become wealthier and the cost of living has risen. Many Italians living in expensive, crowded cities such as Rome and Milan can only afford small apartments without extra rooms for their parents. Many of Rome's elderly now live on their own, with no family to care for or depend on them and without money to live in private homes for the aged.

An Italian wedding reception. Many newly-married Italians try to set up house near their parents.

Even the nuclear family is getting smaller. More Italian women today have jobs outside the home, either for financial independence or to supplement the family income. This often leads to the decision to have fewer babies. Northern Italy registers a significantly lower birth rate than southern Italy, and the national population growth rate ranks among the lowest in Western Europe.

Kids at play.

CHILDHOOD HAS ITS PRIVILEGES

Italian families may be shrinking in size, but parents remain devoted to their children. Italians are generally very affectionate toward children. Parents readily hug and kiss their children in public and will even reach out to touch strangers' children whom they think are beautiful.

Children are regarded as equal members of the household in Italy—they are allowed to express their opinions and are treated as individuals with their own personalities. Italian children are very comfortable with their parents and readily admit (when they are grown up) that they truly love their parents.

Italian parents are ambitious and self-sacrificing for their children without being pushy. They are not likely to encourage their children to learn to read or to play an instrument at a young age. They feel that children will develop these skills in good time if so inclined and should not feel pressure to achieve before they are ready.

Parents also want their children to have what they did not have when they were young. They hold elaborate parties to celebrate their children's birthdays and First Holy Communion day, inviting many guests who arrive with gifts for the child.

ITALIAN MASCULINITY

Italian men pay courteous attention to women, opening doors for them and paying for dinner at restaurants. Traditionally, Italian men headed their families and saw themselves as protector of the women in the household, upholding the honor of their wives, daughters, and mothers. However, the emergence of the nuclear family has gradually altered the balance of power between men and women in the household.

A proud Italian father and his family.

ITALIAN FEMININITY

Italian women are great nurturers, the main source of warmth and affection in the family. They provide the meals for the family, a very important task especially in a food-worshiping culture. They make sure that the children are properly fed and clothed and that they learn good manners and the difference between right and wrong.

Until the 1960s Italian mothers were not encouraged to work outside the home; their lives were focused on looking after the family. Many women were illiterate, because their families did not think it necessary to send them to school.

The 1970s saw a feminist revolution in Italy, as women aggressively pursued equal rights with men under the law. In 1970 divorce was legalized in Italy, despite opposition from the Vatican, and women were

Young Italian women in Rome hold flowers to mark the 2002 World Women's Day.

In the past 55 years, an increasing number of Italian women have taken up jobs traditionally the domain of men.

ensured the right to receive alimony and child support from their former husbands. Abortion was legalized in the late 1970s, a drastic step for a country dominated by Roman Catholics. Italian women can even get government funds to have an abortion.

Italian women gained equal rights in the workplace in 1977. The law ensured that women were paid the same as men in similar jobs. Today working women in Italy are entitled to five months of paid (at 80 percent of their salaries) maternity leave, taken one or two months before delivery and four or three months after. They are entitled to another six months of paid (at 30 percent of their salaries) parental leave, taken before the child turns three. Mothers are also guaranteed the right to return to their jobs before the child reaches his or her first birthday.

Before World War II, few Italian women were employed outside the home or farm. As in many Western nations, most women in Italy today work to help support the family. Italy has a significant proportion of women lawyers, doctors, professors, business managers, and parliament members. About 25 percent of Italy's doctors are women, and 40 percent of the Fiat labor force are women.

Established in the 11th century, the university of Bologna is the oldest institution of higher learning in all of Europe. Many Italian universities are very overcrowded today; the University of Rome has over 160,000 students. Most programs take four years to complete, while degrees in architecture and medicine take five and six years respectively.

EDUCATION

Education is compulsory and free for Italian children aged 6 to 14. Private schools under the ministry of education follow a curriculum similar to that used in public schools.

Mothers who work outside the home may send their toddlers to nursery school or their 5-year-olds to kindergarten. Children aged 6 through 10 must attend *scuola elementare* ("sko-OH-lah eh-leh-men-TAH-reh"), or elementary school. Elementary schoolchildren take subjects such as Italian, mathematics, history, and science. Many elementary schools follow a half-day program six days a week. From ages 11 to 14, all children attend *scuola media* ("MEH-dee-ah"), or middle school. They study more in-depth the same subjects as in elementary school and also take a second language.

After age 14, Italian children can discontinue their education or go on to *liceo* ("LEE-sjeh-oh"), a five-year upper secondary school where they specialize in vocational training or prepare for a university education. Subjects in the vocational program include agriculture, business, and aeronautics. Subjects in the preuniversity program include literature, science, Latin, Greek, philosophy, fine arts, and history. Most middle- and upper-class children choose the path toward university.

ITALIAN WAYS

Certain likes and dislikes, and do's and don'ts offer glimpses of the Italian character:

• Italians are expressive. They tend to gesticulate when talking, especially when bargaining for lower prices in small shops and open markets. Young couples freely display their affection in public.

Football, or soccer, is a national obsession, and Italians are passionate supporters of their favorite clubs. Cycling and basketball are also national sports, but baseball has not caught on.

Italians express themselves most beautifully in the arts; their painting, sculpture, and music have won admirers worldwide.

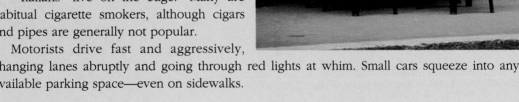

• Italians love food. They take wine and olive oil very seriously; both are basic ingredients in Italian cooking. Extra virgin olive oil also adds flavor to salads, breads, and soups. Alcoholic beverages are served day and night at bars and restaurants (there is no official age limit for buying and drinking alcohol). Getting their first taste of wine at a young age among family, Italians learn to appreciate wine and drink in moderation.

• Italians "live on the edge." Many are habitual cigarette smokers, although cigars and pipes are generally not popular.

Motorists drive fast and aggressively, changing lanes abruptly and going through red lights at whim. Small cars squeeze into any available parking space—even on sidewalks.

Italian students have to study diligently to cope with difficult school examinations held regularly. Secondary school students have to pass a two-day oral and written examination in order to graduate and qualify for admission to university.

RELIGION

THE ANCIENT ROMANS WORSHIPED MANY GODS and incorporated them into a lunar calendar of 355 days. The Romans showed their devotion by building temples dedicated to the gods. Worshipers left offerings of milk, wine, money, jewels, and statues at temple altars and held elaborate public ceremonies and sacrificed animals to win favor from the gods on family matters and for good fortune. Roman cults led by different groups of priests worshiped one or more gods and followed strict rules.

Christianity was born in the first century A.D. among the followers of Jesus of Nazareth. As the religion spread, Roman rulers, especially the emperor Nero, began persecuting Christians. Of all religions that existed in ancient Rome, Christianity was the least tolerated and was banned everywhere in the Roman empire. However, Christianity continued to attract converts until it became the official religion of the empire in the fourth century, when the emperor Constantine saw a vision of a cross in the sky and became a devoted Christian.

From the fall of the Roman empire to the unification of Italy's many city-states in 1870, Roman Catholicism was the strongest force holding the people together. The popes who ruled the Catholic Church had tremendous influence, both spiritual and political, over Italy for centuries. In 1929 Roman Catholicism was made the state religion of Italy. Religious instruction in state schools was mandatory, and the Church had the legal right to censor films, books, and stage plays if they went against Catholic doctrine or portrayed the Church in an unfavorable light.

In 1984 Church and State formally severed ties in an official concordat, although the document reaffirmed the Church's importance in the moral lives of Italians. The Vatican, the home of the pope and center of the worldwide Roman Catholic Church, is located within the city of Rome, although it is a separate sovereign state.

Opposite: **St. Peter's Basilica in Vatican City.**

THE ANCIENT ROMAN GODS

The ancient Romans worshiped a main pantheon of six gods—Apollo, Jupiter, Mars, Mercury, Neptune, and Vulcan—and six goddesses—Ceres, Diana, Juno, Minerva, Venus, and Vesta—led by the Capitoline triad of Jupiter-Juno-Minerva. Most of the Roman gods were in fact Greek gods with Latin names. The Romans admired Greek civilization and adopted many of its elements.

The Romans also adopted gods from other cultures such as Isis from the Egyptian pantheon and Cybele, the Turkish goddess of motherhood. The Capitoline triad was adopted from the Etruscans, who also honored a main pantheon of 12 gods, although the Roman gods are more identified with the Greek gods.

Each god was responsible for a different aspect of the universe. Jupiter, king of the gods, was god of the sky. Juno was the goddess of women, Mercury the god of merchants, Vulcan the god of fire, Mars the god of war, Minerva the goddess of wisdom, and Venus the goddess of fertility and love. After the establishment of the Roman empire, emperors were also worshiped as gods after their death.

RELIGION AND LAW

Roman Catholicism was Italy's strongest unifying force throughout its turbulent history, but since the country's post-World War II economic boom, urbanization and growing prosperity have reduced the influence of religion on the country's politics and laws.

Over the last few decades, the Italian people have decided that they prefer to make their own decisions rather than follow the rules of the Church. In the 1970s, laws were passed legalizing abortion and divorce, both still forbidden by the Roman Catholic Church. Birth control is widely practiced, although the Church also forbids it.

In 1985 a survey found that almost three-fourths of the population did not think that the Church should have anything to do with the country's political system. Catholics have traditionally supported the Christian Democratic Party.

Worshipers in the Sicilian town of Trapani make a solemn procession on Good Friday.

ROMAN CATHOLICISM AND ITALIAN SOCIAL LIFE

The 1985 survey also found that close to half of all Italians did not consider religion a meaningful part of their lives. Church attendance has fallen dramatically. While in smaller towns some people might be motivated to go to church just so the neighbors will not talk, in the cities parishes are so big that people do not notice who attends church and who does not. Changing lifestyles have also affected church attendance. Rural Italians traditionally associate the fertility of the land with devotion to God and the Church, but with fewer people working the land, the significance of religion from this perspective has diminished.

A survey carried out by Italy's national statistics office revealed that in 2000, the Jubilee Year of the Church, only 35 percent of Italian Catholics went to church every week (of which there were twice as many women as men). Of those aged 25 to 34, only 21 percent went to church every week. Some 14 percent polled said that they did not go to church at all. Regular churchgoers in Italy today are generally children, women, the elderly, and rural folk, particularly in the south. Many men who do go to church are farmers, technicians, craftsmen, and clerks. Members of the upper and lower classes do not attend Sunday Mass as often as do members of the middle class.

However, these statistics do not tell the whole story. Although most Italians are not regular churchgoers, many of them place more faith and trust in the Church than they do in the government. Moreover, a great majority still turn to the Church for the important rites of passage in their lives: more than 90 percent are baptized in church and make their first Holy Communion; around 80 percent are confirmed; and nearly all have church weddings. Even members of the Italian Communist Party, which does not encourage religious ties, often participate in these rites.

A ceiling fresco by Raphael in the Vatican. Some of Italy's finest works of art were inspired by the Roman Catholic faith.

Most importantly, the Church sets a moral example for the people. Whether or not modern-day Italians strictly follow the teachings of the Church, the Church helps people to be aware of the difference between right and wrong and of the importance of showing compassion to those in need.

The Church's primary responsibility in Italy today is to help people who are in trouble. The Church provides health and welfare services to the needy, implements programs for prostitutes, the elderly, and drug addicts, and runs homes for the disabled. It also provides employment aid for people who are out of work, food and shelter for the hungry, and of course religious education for children.

The Roman Catholic Church is a tremendous source of pride for the average Italian. The Vatican in Rome is an immensely important institution, the capital of the Roman Catholic world and residence of the pope (the successor of the first leader of the Church, the Apostle Peter). Vatican City contains some of the world's finest art and architecture, including St. Peter's Basilica, one of the country's architectural masterpieces, which attracts millions of visitors every year.

75

VATICAN CITY

Vatican City was granted sovereignty in 1929 by the Lateran Treaty between Mussolini's government and Pope Pius XI. Although Vatican City occupies less than 0.17 square miles (0.44 square km), making it around the size of Central Park in New York City, it is really a fully functioning miniature state within the boundaries of the city of Rome.

The largest and most important structure in Vatican City is St. Peter's Basilica, the world's largest church. The Vatican's colorfully dressed Swiss Guards, trained in martial arts and the use of light weapons for the protection of the pope, make up the world's smallest army.

There are almost 2 million volumes in the Vatican library as well as thousands of Latin, Greek, Arabic, and Hebrew manuscripts, and about 6,000 volumes are added every year. Vatican Radio broadcasts to global audiences in 40 languages, and the Vatican also has its own newspaper, stamps, and prison. Many Nobel Prize winners are members of the Vatican's prestigious Pontifical Academy of Sciences.

MEETING THE POPE

The pope grants a general audience every Wednesday in the piazza of St. Peter's Basilica. When Catholics see him, they shout *"Viva il Papa!"* ("VEE-vah eel PAH-pah"), or "Long live the Pope!"

When meeting the pope in person, worshipers call him either *Santissimo Padre* ("sahn-TEE-see-moh PAH-dray"), which means Holy Father, or *Sua Santita* ("SWAH sahn-TEE-tah"), which means Your Holiness. Former popes (there have been 263) allowed followers to kiss their ring, but Pope John Paul II (*right*), who was elected in 1978, does not care for such expressions of devotion to him.

The pope's official title is Bishop of Rome, Vicar of Jesus Christ, Successor of the Prince of the Apostles, Supreme Pontiff of the Universal Church, Patriarch of the West, Primate of Italy, Archbishop and Metropolitan of the Roman Province, Sovereign of the State of Vatican City, and Servant of the Servants of God.

Catholics aged 16 to 35 around the world have had a chance to meet the pope at the week-long World Youth Day conference held every two years in a different city. Millions of young people, including non-Catholics, have gathered in Rome, Denver, Buenos Aires, Manila, Paris, Toronto, and other cities since the now 81-year-old pope started the event in 1984.

The Vatican is famous for its stunning art treasures: sculptures of the saints by 17th-century artist Gian Lorenzo Bernini atop the giant "arms" encircling the piazza of St. Peter's Basilica; Michelangelo's magnificent *Pietà* sculpture, the Roman sculpture *Apollo Belvedere*, and Raphael's fresco *The Liberation of St. Peter* in the museums; and Michelangelo's famous frescoes, which took four years to paint, covering the 10,000-square-foot (900-square-m) ceiling of the Sistine Chapel.

Some 1,000 people, consisting of cardinals, church officials, altar boys, students, and Swiss Guardsmen, are permanent residents of the Vatican. The most important is the former Cardinal Karol Wojtyla, now Pope John Paul II. He is known for his efforts to unite Catholics around the world through his international travels.

OTHER RELIGIONS AND FOLK BELIEFS

Only about 1 percent of Italians follow other religions. Many of Italy's Protestants belong to the Waldensian Church, started by Peter Waldo in the 12th century in southern France and northern Italy as a reaction against the Roman Catholic Church.

Jews make up the other significant non-Catholic group in Italy. Some are descended from families who lived in Rome as far back as the pre-Christian era, others came from Spain in the 15th century, and still others came from Germany and Poland in the late 19th and early 20th centuries. Most of the Jewish community is centered in Milan and Rome, while Florence and Trieste have small congregations. An old Jewish neighborhood—synagogues and kosher restaurant intact—still survives in Rome.

THE LEGEND OF ROMULUS AND REMUS

According to ancient Roman legend, Rome was founded in 753 B.C. by Romulus who was abandoned with his twin brother Remus near the Tiber River in Rome when they were babies.

The twins' mother was the virgin princess Rhea Silvia, who had been raped by Mars, the god of war. The babies were saved by a female wolf—who allowed

them to suckle her for milk—and brought up by a shepherd. When Romulus grew up, he decided to build a city on the spot where he had been saved. According to ancient Roman writings, Romulus marked out the four corners of the city, plowed a ditch from corner to corner to delineate the city boundaries, and built a wall to fortify the area.

In 1990 Italian archeologist Andrea Carandini set out to prove that the myth of Rome's founding was based on truth. By digging 20 feet (6 m) under the Palatine, one of the seven hills of Rome, Carandini uncovered the wall he believed to be the one erected by Romulus. Nearby, he found pottery dating back to about 730 B.C., further evidence that Rome was founded during the time of Romulus. In fact, Rome is believed to be named after Romulus. The statue showing the baby brothers suckling from a she-wolf (*above*) dates back to Etruscan times. Unfortunately, Carandini had to discontinue his search due to lack of financial support.

Muslims, mostly students and immigrants from Hungary, Albania, Bulgaria, and Slovenia, make up another religious group in Italy. Other minority groups include the Buddhists and Baha'is.

Many Italians, particularly in the southern regions, still maintain folk beliefs. Some women in small villages are said to have magical powers. They are consulted for potions or charms to win the hearts of lovers, for predictions about the future, or for lottery numbers. Some southerners fear witches and actually perform animal sacrifices to keep them away.

LANGUAGE

ITALIAN IS A ROMANCE LANGUAGE descended from the Vulgar Latin dialect spoken by people living in the last years of the Roman empire. Italian uses more Latin words than do other Romance languages such as Spanish and French, and it has a similar grammatical structure to that of Latin. Latin is still the language of Vatican City in Rome; official papal documents are printed in Latin as well as seven other languages.

Italian is one of the most melodic and expressive languages in the world. Although Italians use their language eloquently and dramatically, they do not demand that foreigners speak it as well as they do. Italian is spoken by more than 65 million people in Italy, Switzerland, the United States, Canada, Argentina, and Brazil.

Opposite: **Italian newspapers use the dialect of Tuscany.**

OFFICIAL AND STANDARD ITALIAN

Official Italian used in business and the mass media is the dialect of Tuscany (of Florence, to be precise), recognized throughout Italy as the purest dialect and most cultured accent. However, standard Italian leans more toward the dialect of Rome.

The Tuscan dialect became influential in the late 13th and early 14th centuries when Florence was at its political and cultural peak. Tuscan authors such as Dante, Giovanni Boccaccio, and Francesco Petrarca began to use their dialect in literary works.

Between the Renaissance and the mid-20th century, most Italians still spoke regional dialects. Only the educated upper classes both wrote and spoke "pure" Italian. Regional dialects caused communication problems among soldiers from different regions during World War I.

After World War II, the Tuscan dialect became more standardized and was taught in schools. The literacy rate rose, and people became familiar with official Italian through emerging communication media.

Dialects are still spoken by older Italians but are fading away among the younger generations.

REGIONAL DIALECTS

Other than the Tuscan and Roman dialects, many more regional dialects are spoken in Italy such as Venetian, Aostan, Ligurian, Napoletano, Milanese, Corsican, and Occitan in the Piedmontese provinces of Cuneo and Turin. On the island of Sardinia alone, there are four different dialects, and there are also several Sicilian dialects.

Speaking a dialect is not the same as speaking with an accent. A dialect is a language variety with its own grammar and vocabulary. In Italy, some dialects are so drastically dissimilar that two people speaking two different dialects may not be able to understand each other. In contrast, people from different regions in the United States or England may speak with different accents and still be able to understand one another.

Many young Italians speak a dialect at home to their parents and grandparents, but converse in standard Italian when outside the home. Dialect is still the primary means of communication in small agricultural towns or villages and on small islands.

One reason why Italian dialects are so varied is that political unity is a recent reality in the country. Another reason is the geography of the landscape, isolating one region from another and allowing each dialect to flourish on its own. Many Italian dialects have been influenced by the languages of neighboring countries or of invaders who laid claim to the land at some point in the country's history.

While most Italian dialects have Latin roots, the Aostan dialect is said to sound more like French, Venetian is sprinkled with Spanish and Portuguese words, and Piedmontese has a good deal of German. Southern

Italian dialects have a Greek influence. Fortunately, most dialects when written can be understood by any Italian speaker.

THE INFLUENCE OF ITALIAN AND VICE VERSA

During the Renaissance and the following centuries, Italy had an important influence on the cultures of France and England. Many Italian words made their way into the everyday speech of the French and the English, and many of these words have become so common in modern usage that few people recognize their Italian roots.

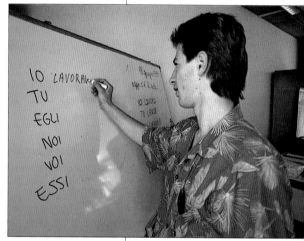

"I work, you work, he works ..." the fundamentals of learning Italian grammar would be familiar to someone studying English grammar.

Numerous words that relate to music come from Italian: libretto, maestro, mandolin, piano, soprano, and tempo. Food words include broccoli, cappuccino, espresso, minestrone, and salami. Military terms such as battalion, cavalry, and colonel have been adapted from Italian.

Italian words used in English with the exact same spelling include fiasco, fresco, ghetto, incognito, motto, solo, studio, and trio. And then of course there is *ciao* ("CHAOW"), the word Italians use to say both "hello" and "goodbye," which has been readily adopted by many other cultures. Words such as balcony, cartoon, sonnet, and zany originate in 16th-century Italian. Other English words borrowed or adapted from Italian include arcade, regatta, umbrella, and vendetta.

In the opposite direction, English words have also found their way into Italian, especially since World War II. Some examples are supermarket, or *supermercato* ("soo-per-mer-KAH-toh") in Italian, popcorn, shopping, TV, poster, weekend, party, jeans, and cameraman.

ITALIAN SAYINGS AND THEIR ENGLISH EQUIVALENTS

Some of the ideas behind common English sayings and proverbs are also expressed in Italian using different words:

Italian: You're speaking Turkish.
English: It's Greek to me.

Italian: When the cat is out, the mice are dancing.
English: When the cat's away, the mice will play.

Italian: Better an egg today than a chicken tomorrow.
English: A bird in the hand is worth two in the bush.

Italian: Much smoke but a small roast.
English: Much ado about nothing.

Italian: Drop by drop the sea is filled.
English: Little drops of water make the mighty ocean.

BODY LANGUAGE

Spoken Italian is said to be extremely expressive and persuasive. The dramatic gestures that Italians are famous for give the verbal language a new dimension.

HAND PURSE Probably the most characteristic Italian gesture (and the one most used by actors playing Italians), the hand purse consists of the fingers and thumb pointing upward, tips meeting to form a pocket or purse. To Italians, the hand purse indicates a question, such as "What are you doing?", "What do you want?", or "What do you mean?" In a tense situation such as a traffic jam in Rome, an irritated Italian might lean out of his car window and hand purse forward to ask the person in the car in front of him, "What is going on?"

THUMBS UP This gesture was used by ancient Roman emperors in the Colosseum to indicate that a gladiator who had fought hard but lost should

Close friends and relatives exchange hugs and kisses when greeting.

not be killed. (Thumbs down meant that the gladiator had to die.) Centuries later, the thumbs up was reintroduced to Italians as an "okay" sign by American soldiers in World War II. Another American gesture meaning "okay," a ring made with the thumb and forefinger, means "zero" or "the pits" to northern Italians. To southern Italians, it is a major insult.

HANDSHAKE This is the standard greeting gesture for acquaintances. The average Italian who runs into someone he or she knows on the street will stop, shake hands, and chat, even if in a hurry, then shake hands again before moving on.

CHEEK SCREW Another typically Italian gesture, the cheek screw consists of the tip of the forefinger pressing into the cheek and making a screwing motion. This gesture is mainly used to indicate praise or to imply that something is especially good or beautiful. It is often used to compliment a good meal.

Italian students on a trip to the Vatican. Education in Italy is conducted in the Tuscan dialect.

OTHER GESTURES Like almost everything in Italy, gestures have different interpretations in different regions. To a Neapolitan, pulling your eyelid is a warning to be alert; elsewhere in Italy, it might mean that someone is sly or cunning. In Rome and Naples, tapping the side of your nose is a friendly warning, while in Sardinia it indicates a shared secret. To flick your chin with your hand is a strong dismissive gesture meaning "I couldn't care less." In the south, however, it is interpreted as a simple, emotionless "no."

PERSONAL SPACE Italians have few inhibitions about personal space and standing close to one another. They are rarely self-conscious about embracing, and it is not unusual to see two men kissing each other on both cheeks. For both men and women, walking *a fracetto* ("ah frah-CHEH-toh"), or arm-in-arm, simply shows friendship. Many younger Italians stand up to show respect when an older family member or friend walks into the room.

TITLES

Signore ("se-NYOH-reh") and *Signora* ("se-NYOH-rah") are the Italian equivalents of "Mr." and "Madam" or "Mrs." It is considered impolite in Italy to call an older person or a mere acquaintance by his or her first name until a firmer relationship has been established.

It is proper to show deference and respect for an engineer, doctor, lawyer, or professor by addressing him or her by the appropriate professional title: *Ingegnere* ("en-jeh-NYEH-reh"), *Dottore* ("doh-TOH-reh"), *Avvocato* ("ah-voh-KAH-toh"), and *Professore* ("pro-feh-SOH-reh") respectively. *Don* and *Donna* are used before the first name of a person who has made an outstanding achievement or for whom one wants to show great respect.

OTHER LANGUAGES AND DIALECTS

Although Tuscan is taught in all the schools and is the official Italian language, some 5 percent of the population still use their own dialects.

People of German heritage living in Trentino-Alto Adige, or South Tyrol, speak German as well as Italian. Other inhabitants of South Tyrol also speak Ladin, an ancient language similar to Romansh, one of the four national languages of Switzerland. In Valle d'Aosta, about three-quarters of the inhabitants speak a French dialect. Some 50,000 people living in Piedmont speak Provençal, also a French dialect. Catalan, which is similar to Provençal, has been spoken in Sardinia since the 14th century.

Greek dialects are spoken in parts of Apulia. In Friuli-Venezia Giulia, which borders Slovenia and Austria, some ethnic groups speak Croat, Slovene, and German. Some communities in Calabria and Sicily speak Albanian. A small community of Armenians on the island of San Lazzaro in Venice speak their own language. Gypsies in the north use the Sinthi dialect, while those in central and southern Italy use the Rom dialect.

In the 1930s and 1940s, Mussolini's fascist regime tried to force ethnic groups into a national culture by eliminating foreign words from Italian. The campaign also included inventing new words to replace English ones. Donald Duck turned into Paperino, Mickey Mouse became Topolino, and Goofy was Pippo. In soccer, "goal" became meta. *These linguistic inventions have now disappeared from Italian.*

ARTS

ITALY HAS INSPIRED THE WORLD for centuries with its remarkable artistic accomplishments. The ancient Romans were skilled engineers who built impressive monuments throughout their far-reaching empire. Italy was the birthplace of the Renaissance, the era that marked the transition from medieval to modern times and produced a great revival in architecture, sculpture, painting, and literature. The ancient Romans invented the aqueduct and amphitheater, and Italy later gave the world the *Mona Lisa* and *David*; Dante's *The Divine Comedy*; the Verdi and Puccini operas; the plays of Nobel Prize winner Luigi Pirandello; the novels of Alberto Moravia, Italo Calvino, Umberto Eco, and Elsa Morante; and the films of Federico Fellini, Bernardo Bertolucci, and Liliana Cavani.

For more than 300 years, people from all over the world have flocked to Italy to see its art treasures, including 30,000 Roman Catholic churches and 20,000 castles. Many well-known novelists and poets, escaping to Italy from their own more conservative cultures, have written eloquently about their experience: Charles Dickens, Henry James, Mark Twain, Herman Melville, E.M. Forster, D.H. Lawrence; John Keats, Percy Shelley, Lord Byron, Goethe, and John Milton.

Below: **Michelangelo's David.**

Opposite: **Shimmering Greek-Byzantine mosaics cover the interior of the 12th-century Palatine Chapel in Palermo, Sicily.**

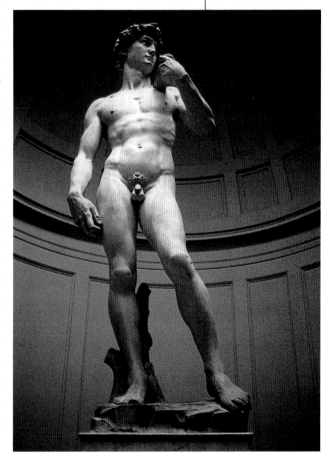

Italians rest at Bernini's Fountain of the Four Rivers in Rome's Piazza Navona.

ART HISTORY IN MODERN LIFE

Millions of art lovers visit Italy to stroll in art museums in Florence, climb the steps of the Colosseum in Rome, marvel at Michelangelo's restored frescoes on the ceiling of the Sistine Chapel in the Vatican, and wonder at the magnificence of Leonardo da Vinci's original *The Last Supper* in Milan.

Italy is said to have more artistic masterpieces per square mile than any other country in the world. Many Italians see their country's art treasures everyday without having to enter a museum. Examples of ancient and Renaissance architecture mingle with modern structures. Children play in *piazza* crowned by ornate baroque fountains, and people worship in churches filled with art that is fit for the world's finest museums.

THE RENAISSANCE

In the entire history of Italian art (which continues in the present), the greatest contribution was made during the Renaissance, with enormous artistic and intellectual insights that brought the 15th and 16th centuries out of the obscure Middle Ages and put the ancient Greco-Roman civilizations as well as Christianity into totally new perspectives. The Italian Renaissance is traditionally divided into three main phases, or generations: early, high, and late.

EARLY RENAISSANCE The Early Renaissance began in the early 15th century in Florence, where artists began to study the ancient Greeks and adopted their ideas about classical form and proportion. Renaissance artists portrayed the human body in an ideal or heroic manner, with a well-proportioned figure in a flattering position and showing emotion.

Filippo Brunelleschi (1377–1446) was the leading architect of this period. Using the classic Roman architectural principles of harmony and balance, he built the first Renaissance building, a hospital in Florence. His masterpiece, the dome of the Santa Maria del Fiore church in Florence, is considered the highest achievement of Renaissance architecture.

The sculptor Donatello (1386–1466) created beautiful, realistic statues of religious heroes, thus reviving the long-neglected style of the freestanding statue. Tommaso Cassai (1401–28), known as Masaccio, was the most notable painter of the Early Renaissance. He often derived his subject matter from ancient Rome, and his frescoes were remarkable for their use of perspective and their idealization of the human form.

Sandro Botticelli (1446–1510) is well-known for his detailed painting *The Birth of Venus,* which depicts the goddess of love rising from the sea. Piero della Francesca (1416–92) filled his light-tone frescoes with graceful figures of exact proportions.

The spirit of the Renaissance achieved its sharpest formulation in art, which was seen as a branch of knowledge capable of providing humankind with images of God and His creations and with insights into humankind's position in the universe.

91

Raphael's *School of Athens* in the Vatican depicts Plato, Aristotle, and other great philosophers of ancient Greece.

HIGH RENAISSANCE The High Renaissance, in the first part of the 16th century, was Italy's most creative artistic period, producing such artists as Leonardo da Vinci (1452–1519), Michelangelo Buonarotti (1475–1564), and Raffaello Sanzio (1483–1520), known as Raphael, and the architect Donato Bramante (1444–1514).

Artists were able to work on a grand scale due to the financial support they received from Italy's leading families such as the Medici of Florence and the Sforza of Milan. The Roman Catholic Church was also a great patron of the arts, wishing to fill the Vatican with important works of art and turn it into a magnificent monument to God. The colors and textures of the paintings of the High Renaissance are particularly dramatic, due to the use of oil paints rather than egg-based tempera.

Da Vinci painted one of his finest works during the High Renaissance. *The Last Supper* depicts Christ's last meal, when he tells his disciples that he knows he will be betrayed. Da Vinci believed in "paint[ing] the face in such a way that it will be easy to understand what is going on in the mind" and so gave each of the disciples a different facial expression.

Bramante was commissioned by Pope Julius III to rebuild St. Peter's Church in Rome, today the world's largest church. Many of the church's paintings and sculptures were done by Michelangelo. In his Sistine Chapel frescoes of God and Adam and his monumental sculptures of Moses and David, Michelangelo created powerful figures recognized by people around the world. While Michelangelo was painting the Sistine Chapel, Raphael painted several masterpieces on the walls of the papal rooms (now part of the Vatican museums). *School of Athens* in the Stanza della Segnatura is considered Raphael's greatest work.

Titian's *Venus of Urbino*.

The High Renaissance was represented in Venice by the painters Giorgione, Titian, Tintoretto, and Veronese and the architect Andrea Palladio, who built classical villas for the wealthy on the outskirts of the city and later inspired great international architects.

LATE RENAISSANCE During the latter part of the 16th century, a new style of painting, Mannerism, evolved. Mannerism refers to the highly stylized works of artists such as Pontormo and Parmigianino, who used strong colors and unnaturally elongated and emotionless figures, very different from the emotional, idealized subjects of earlier Renaissance painters. Mannerism was followed by the more elaborate baroque style in the early 17th century. Baroque definitively replaced the Renaissance aesthetic ideal with a more dramatic, asymmetrical style. Noted baroque artists included Caravaggio, the Carracci family, and Bernini.

ART RESTORATION IN ITALY

Many of the world's masterpieces in Italy are in disrepair. Exposure to the climate and human activity has caused them to wear and tear, fade and flake. In the chapels, centuries of burning oil lamps and candles have coated the art on the walls with soot.

Massive efforts began in the late 20th century to try to restore Italy's art treasures to their former glory. Fine-art restoration has become a major profession, and there are schools that train people to become restorers of ceramics, paintings, buildings, and sculptures. Yet, even with the help of modern technology to map out in detail every inch of an original painting, restoration is still a painstaking and time-consuming effort.

Restorers took four times as long to restore *The Last Supper* as it took da Vinci to paint it. The restoration effort, concluded in 1999, not only restored colors dulled by humidity, dust, and pollution since the original was finished in 1498, but repaired damage done in previous restoration attempts.

The Leaning Tower of Pisa (*above*) began to lean soon after it was built in the 12th century because of sandy foundations. The tower continued to lean slightly more every year until in 1990, in danger of collapsing, the tower was closed. It took almost 12 years and US$25 million to correct the incline of the centuries-old tower before it could finally be reopened to tourists in 2001. Now only 30 people are allowed to climb the tower at any time. The next step in the restoration project is to clean the tower's facade of grime.

Italians are concerned about the deterioration of their country's art treasures. In the major cities, vehicle emissions and movement have damaged many monuments. In Rome, vibrations from road traffic have caused whole sections of marble to fall off some ancient monuments. In 1986 floods in Venice brought 5 feet (1.5 m) of water into *piazzas*, museums, and churches, soiling beautiful mosaics and paintings.

Unfortunately, there are just too many art treasures in need of restoration for the national government to finance all of them. Often, corporations and local governments donate money to support projects that are given priority.

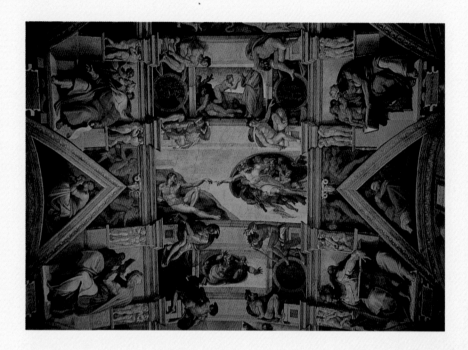

One major restoration project that attracted a great deal of attention was the restoration of Michelangelo's frescoes on the ceiling of the Sistine Chapel (*above*). A Japanese television network, Nippon Television, donated $3 million to the project in exchange for exclusive rights to film the process.

As restorers cleaned away layers of soot from centuries of burning candles and the grease used by former restorers to impede cracking, the original colors of the paintings began to show. This "discovery" was very significant, for contrary to the somber shades (deep grays, dark maroons, and earthy olives) and subtle shadows that Michelangelo's work had been known for, the colors of his most famous work proved to be loud and gaudy: neon purple, electric green and yellow, and glowing pink. Centuries of dirt had toned down the colors, giving them an earthy appearance.

Some art historians claim that the restorers went too far in their cleaning efforts, that in removing the years of accumulated grime they also removed the dark shadows that Michelangelo had intended. According to Italian art critic Giovanni Carandente, "Michelangelo must be studied all over again, so revolutionary is this discovery about the painter of whom some had dared to write that in the Sistine he adopted colors that all leaned to brick or gray."

THE OPERA

Italy has contributed tremendously to the development of Western music. European opera originated in Italy, and the Italian language provided the world with a musical vocabulary.

Musicians and poets in Florence began setting poems to music in the late 16th century. The first operas were produced in the early 17th century in Rome, Venice, and Naples. As the passion for opera swept the country, each city developed its own style. Claudio Monteverdi (1567–1643), considered the father of modern opera, led the Venetian school of composers. Alessandro Scarlatti (1660–1725) wrote nearly 100 operas and made Naples an operatic center. Leading European composers such as German-born George Frideric Handel (1685–1759) traveled to Italy to study opera. Even Mozart (1756–91) composed for Milan's La Scala, Europe's most famous opera house, which opened in 1778.

The Archimboldi Theater in Milan, designed by Vittorio Gregotti with a seating capacity of 2,400, was opened in January 2002. It will serve as the provisional location of the La Scala opera house while the original building is renovated.

In 1816 Gioachino Antonio Rossini (1792–1868) composed the classic comic opera *The Barber of Seville*. Giuseppe Verdi (1813–1901), one of Italy's finest composers, wrote 26 operas including *Rigoletto*, *La Traviata*, *Il Trovatore*, and *Aida* (set in Egypt and often performed with live animals such as camels). Known for their dramatic plots, his operas often dwell on the struggle of the oppressed. Giacomo Puccini (1858–1924) was another major 19th-century composer. His *La Boheme* and *Madame Butterfly* are well-loved for their romantic, moving stories and melodies.

Opera first catered to the upper classes. The opening of the public opera house in Venice in 1637 made it a source of entertainment for everyone. Crowds filled the halls on opening night and discussed the performance for days after. Even today, Italians may talk during the performance; some get very involved with the action on stage and offer their comments to others around them.

A performance at the famed summer opera in the Roman amphitheater in Verona.

ITALIAN COMEDY

The Renaissance developed a new style of theater called the *commedia dell'arte* ("kom-MAY-diah del LAHR-teh"). This was basically improvised drama, although in actual practice the plays, divided into acts and scenes, were conceived and rehearsed in advance. Although the actors could still add their personal spontaneous touches to their parts, they needed to do so with clarity and wit.

Commedia dell'arte often addressed earthy issues and followed simple plots, such as how an unlikely couple fall in love or how a member of the lower class manages to trick a rich nobleman. The actors played stock characters, such as Arlecchino the servant, Scarramuccia the adventurer, Inamorato the lover, Pantalone the clown, Columbina the lady's maid, Mezzetino the musician, and Pedrolino the dreamer. There were no elaborate sets, and props included animals, furniture, and weapons.

Commedia dell'arte actors raised the standards of the art—they were Europe's first professional actors. They worked hard to blend their parts and to deliver the right words at the right time. They did not only act, but also sang, danced, fenced, did somersaults, and told jokes, and the audience laughed, cried, and gave their comments and suggestions as the characters got into and out of all kinds of trouble.

This theatrical style was often performed by traveling troupes around the country and was initially meant for a very popular audience. It was excluded from performances for the clergy or the higher society at royal courts until in the 16th century, when a *commedia dell'arte* troupe from Italy visited Catherine de Medici in France. The style later influenced the farces of the French playwright Molière (who adapted a few of the Italian characters) and left its mark in the French pantomime. *Commedia dell'arte* also became popular in England, Germany, and Russia and even today is seen at theater festivals in Europe.

The Italian comic opera, or opera buffa, originated in Naples in the 18th century, It developed from the interludes that were performed between acts in serious operas.

FLORENCE—CITY OF CRAFTSPEOPLE

Many Italian cities and towns are renowned for their craftsmanship: Cremona in Lombardy for its master violin-makers; Carrara in Tuscany for its marble-cutters; Murano near Venice for its glasswork; and nearby Burano for its lacework.

But Florence is most associated with centuries of expert craftsmanship. Its narrow, winding streets are lined by tiny shops where generations of fine artisans have perfected their skills. Certain workshops are devoted to silversmiths who create intricate figures and make jewelry to order. There are also woodcarvers who both carve items for sale and do expert restoration work in Florence's Renaissance churches. Metal sculptors, framemakers, and artisans also work in copper, bronze, and marble.

Many craftspeople in Florence work with leather and gold. Goldsmiths' workshops have historically been located in the buildings on Florence's oldest bridge, the Ponte Vecchio (*above*). There are even a few silkweavers who still work on a type of loom designed by Leonardo da Vinci. To create a length of fabric, the weaver threads each strand into the loom by hand, quite a job since the pattern consists of 40,000 strands. Many silkweavers are women whose mothers and grandmothers also wove silk in the same workshop.

LITERATURE

Before the 13th century, Italian writers composed in Latin, the formal language for literary purposes. In the 13th century, a group of poets at the court of Frederick II started writing in Tuscan, the dialect of Florence. Among the most famous writers of this time was Dante Alighieri (1265–1321). His most important work, *The Divine Comedy*, has greatly influenced Italian literature and is still considered the single finest work written in that language.

The Divine Comedy is an epic poetic work describing the journey through hell, purgatory, and heaven. The poet adopts a different voice in each part to match the mood of the place he is describing. Along the way, he meets the souls of both the sinners and the saved and, threatened by both sides, illustrates the difficulty of choosing the right path.

The Divine Comedy discusses important issues such as politics and its evils, various kinds of love, the nature of free will, and religious salvation. The work is an amazing exhibition of the length and breadth of Dante's knowledge and an important historical document about the Middle Ages.

Together with Dante, two writers marked the beginnings of Italian literature: Francesco

Petrarca (1304–74), best known for his collection of Italian verses, *Canzoniere*, also called *Petrarch's Sonnets*, inspired by his love interest Laura; and the more entertaining Giovanni Boccaccio (1313–75), whose *Decamerone* ("deh-kahm-meh-ROH-neh") is a collection of short, distinctly permissive, and realistic stories.

THE ARTS IN MODERN ITALY

Italian artists continued to make a significant impact in the 20th century, when many avant-garde movements emerged throughout Europe. Nobel Prize-winning playwright Luigi Pirandello (1867–1936) and the writers Italo Calvino, Oriana Fallaci, Elsa Morante, Alberto Moravia, and Ignazio Silone received international attention for their works.

Umberto Eco's novels —*The Name of the Rose*, a detective story set in a monastery in the Middle Ages, and *Foucault's Pendulum*, on the human condition—have sold millions of copies.

Other Italian artists include sculptor-painter Amedeo Modigliani, known for his elegant elongated portraits; surrealist painter Giorgio de Chirico; and opera singer Luciano Pavarotti.

Below: **A sidewalk caricaturist. Struggling artists and art students paint for tourists to make ends meet.**

Opposite: **Dante wrote *The Divine Comedy* in exile between 1310 and 1321.**

LEISURE

ITALIAN SUNDAYS are typically spent on leisure activities. Many Italians go to cafés, where they chat with old friends over coffee or wine, discuss politics, or argue passionately about the strengths and weaknesses of local soccer heroes. Italian cafés allow, even encourage, their customers to stay as long as they like. Customers can read quietly, write letters, or meet friend after friend at the same table for hours without feeling any pressure to leave.

If it is a fair Sunday, an Italian family may enjoy an extended lunch at an outdoor restaurant, talking about how good the food and wine are and, more importantly, discussing a variety of topics. Young Italians meet their friends at the local beach or a *piazza* in the city to just hang out.

THE PASSEGGIATA

The *passeggiata* ("pah-say-JAH-tah"), or evening stroll, is one of Italy's most enduring, civilized leisure activities. Every evening before dinner in many towns, people dress up and stroll in the main square, greeting one another as they meet and chatting amicably about the day's events. Some sit near the sidewalks at cafés and watch passers-by.

The *passeggiata* gives Italians a chance to look their best and to see their neighbors dressed up as well. It is an avenue for them to touch base with fellow members of the community and to catch up on what has been going on in their neighborhood.

Above and opposite: Italians enjoy the simple things in life such as taking a walk, eating a meal, and watching the world go by.

SOCCER MANIA

A passion for *calcio* ("KAHL-choh"), or soccer, is the strongest factor unifying Italy's competing regions. For many Italians, Sunday begins at church, after which the family has lunch together and then gathers in front of the television set to watch a soccer match.

Soccer is more than a sport or a business in Italy. Some fans may say that it is a part of living, like breathing! Of the three concerns most important to many Italian men (women, food, and soccer), the last takes precedence on the day of a big game.

Soccer was introduced to Italians in the late 1800s by the British, but it was not until the 1930s, under Mussolini, that the sport took off on an international level. Mussolini believed that a great Italian soccer team would be a source of national pride, and he saw to it that stadiums were built and teams nurtured all over the country.

Italy has had championship-winning teams ever since and has won the World Cup three times, the last in 1982. In 1990, as host, Italy beat England to win the bronze match. After that, however, the European soccer giant faced a string of losses: to Brazil in the 1994 finals in the United States, to host France in the 1998 quarter finals, and in 2002 to host Korea in the second round.

Italian children start playing soccer at an early age. A game can start anywhere—in a public square, on a small street, in the schoolyard—and any time. Italians follow the big soccer leagues with passion. There are 16 Series A, or First Division, teams that play one another for the national title. The winner plays other national teams in European and international games. Soccer stories dominate the headlines of Italy's three sports daily newspapers—*La Gazzetta dello Sport, Corriere dello Sport - Stadio,* and *Tuttosport*—and its weekly sports magazine *Guerin Sportivo.*

Italians are fiercely loyal to their city's soccer team. Some of the best Italian teams are Rome's SS Lazio and AS Roma, AC Milan (owned by Prime Minister Silvio Berlusconi), Turin's Juventus (owned by Fiat president Gianni Agnelli), and AC Fiorentina from Florence.

Italy's star players from past and present include Roberto Baggio, Paolo Rossi, Paolo Maldini, Dino Zoff, Salvatore Schillaci, Giuseppe Meazza, and Gianni Rivera. Italy also imports some of the finest players from other countries.

The victories and losses of their favorite teams can make Italians very exhilarated or very angry. Italian soccer fans have a reputation for being rowdy and uninhibited in voicing their opinions about players, especially those not playing up to par. If a player gets hurt, fans are likely to call him "faker," "exaggerator," or even "old man." When the national team came home from their 1986 World Cup defeat, fans met the players at the airport—not to help soothe their wounds, but to boo them! When a team wins, fans are likely to rush onto the field and rip the shirts off the players.

Soccer fans—in Italy called *tifosi* ("te-FOH-se"), which literally means typhus carriers—have been known to stir up violence at stadiums. The worst occurrence was at the 1985 European Cup, when 39 fans, mainly Italian, died in a brawl at the stadium in Belgium.

A big turnout for a soccer match. Italian soccer fans are passionately involved with the game and can reach heights of ecstasy or become absolutely despondent depending on whether their team wins or loses.

BASEBALL

Italians learned to play baseball from Americans stationed in Italy after World War II. Popular among Italian youth, the game is also played professionally, although Italian baseball professionals are not paid nearly as well as their counterparts on professional soccer teams, and the level of play is not up to that of American baseball. Many of Italy's professional baseball players come from the United States, some from the minor leagues and others as retirees from the major leagues.

Contemporary baseball in Italy has been likened to 1940s and 1950s baseball in the United States. Baseball stadiums in Italy are generally smaller and more intimate than those in the United States, and families bring picnic baskets to watch the game together. The oldest stadium in Nettuno, just south of Rome, has very limited seating in the stands, with a capacity of only 1,200. However, some 4,000 people usually squeeze in for the games. The fans, like those for soccer, are extremely devoted and unhesitatingly vocal, but rarely violent.

BASKETBALL

Basketball is fast gaining popularity among Italian children. Many watch the American NBA games on television, and some of the most devoted attend expensive basketball camps in the summer. Basketball is still an amateur sport in Italy. Teams play according to amateur rules, thereby qualifying them to compete in the Olympics. Players do, however, take home excellent salaries and are allowed to have commercial sponsorship. Italian basketball players are often coached by Americans, and the best ones are sent to the United States to play on college teams with the promise that they will return to help the team at home.

Participants in the Tour of Italy.

OTHER OUTDOOR PURSUITS

Italians take part in amateur sports such as horseback riding, running, cycling, swimming, boating, and tennis. During summer vacations, families rent beach or mountain cottages or go to their country villas. Skiing is popular in the winter months. There are ski slopes a few hours' drive from Rome, but the best skiing is found in the Italian Alps and the Dolomites. People living in small towns enjoy a relaxing type of lawn bowling called *bocce* ("BOH-chay").

Italians follow professional cycling and car racing with great interest. Italy's biggest cycling race is the *Giro d'Italia*, or Tour of Italy. The annual marathon, covering more than 2,000 miles (3,218 km), attracts the world's best riders. Italians have won the race consistently since 1997; in 2002 Paolo Savoldelli beat American Tyler Hamilton by less than two minutes.

The Italian Grand Prix takes the Formula One race onto the Monza circuit 9 miles (15 km) northeast of Milan.

Cinema poster artist Silvano Campeggi poses with one of his works at a retrospective exhibition.

TELEVISION

Italians are avid television viewers. From being basically a large-city phenomenon more than 20 years ago, television has today penetrated the country's most remote villages.

In addition to the public terrestrial network, Radiotelevisione Italiana (RAI), which runs four channels, Italy has around eight private national channels, three pay-television channels, and a multitude of cable and satelite channels.

While Italian news, sports, and entertainment programs are traditional favorites, North American shows have become the rage. Italians love soap operas and game shows.

MOVIES AND MUSIC

The golden year for Italian film was 1955 when people bought more than 800 million cinema tickets to see Italian-made westerns (spaghetti westerns) and epics. Ticket sales have since dwindled to less than 100 million a year, only about half the original number of movie theaters remain, and fewer movies are made every year.

Italians still love movies, but the teenagers—the ones who go to the cinema the most—seem to prefer Hollywood productions. Their parents, however, prefer watching movies at home to paying for the big screen experience. To cater to the latter audience, some Italian directors make two versions of their films: one a full-length feature; the other divided into episodes to fit the mini-series television format.

Italy's most famous directors include Roberto Rossellini (1906–77), Federico Fellini (1920–93), Franco Zeffirelli (*The Taming of the Shrew, Hamlet*), Bernardo Bertolucci (*The Last Emperor*), and Giuseppe Tornatore (*Cinema Paradiso*). Rossellini first gained international recognition in 1946 with *Open City*, while Fellini made his international breakthrough with *La Strada* in 1954.

Opera is big in Italy. Italians are serious opera lovers and feel proud to live in the country where opera was born. Venice, Naples, and Milan are the main centers, and there are free concerts of chamber or symphonic music in cities and towns throughout the year.

THE READING PUBLIC

Libraries and bookstores abound in many of Italy's cities, but Italians generally do not read as many books as do their northern European neighbors. Italians do, however, spend a good deal of time reading newspapers and magazines.

Most of the nation's newspapers are published in the north, and each major city has one or two dailies with large circulations. Each major political party publishes a daily paper, as does the Vatican. Sports newspapers and magazines are extremely popular, as are illustrated weeklies that focus on women's topics, religion, politics, business, and popular culture.

The writing style of many of Italy's most respected papers is said to be notoriously highbrow and directed toward the intellectual reader. Italian journalists tend to digress and do not hesitate to offer their own idiosyncratic opinions before describing the actual events. Many Italian newspapers have entire sections dedicated to literary and cultural issues, polemics, and criticism.

The opening night at Milan's famous opera house, La Scala, usually in the first week of December, is one of the most exciting social and cultural events of the year. Opera lovers show up in black tie or long gowns, having bought their tickets weeks, sometimes months, in advance.

109

FESTIVALS

ITALIANS RELISH CELEBRATION, a time for colorful parades and processions. The number of annual festivals in Italy is staggering; one takes place somewhere in the country almost everyday. This after the government decided in the 1970s that there were too many festivals and abolished seven, including St. Valentine's Day.

Tradition is deeply ingrained in Italian culture. Italian festivals are mostly religious or historical. Many religious festivals honor saints. There are patron saints for different professions and special favors. Towns and villages also have their own patron saints and, on the saint's feast day, the inhabitants put on traditional clothes, play traditional music, and parade a large statue of the saint through the streets.

The historical festivals honor great events (many dating back to the Middle Ages or the Renaissance), on a national, regional, or local level. Such celebrations usually include a reenactment of the event, a costumed procession, and sometimes a mock battle or contest such as a horse race, ball game, or boat race.

Opposite: **An Easter Sunday marching band.**

NATIONAL HOLIDAYS AND MAJOR CITY FEAST DAYS

New Year's Day: January 1
Epiphany: January 6
Easter Monday: late March/early April
Liberation Day (national); Feast of St. Mark (Venice): April 25
Labor Day: May 1
Republic Day: June 2
Feast of St. John the baptist (Florence): June 24

Feast of St. Peter and St. Paul (Rome): June 29
Assumption: August 15
All Saints' Day: November 1
Feast of St. Ambrose (Milan): December 7
Immaculate Conception: December 8
Christmas: December 25
St. Stephen's Day: December 26

Assisi celebrates the colorful *Calendimaggio* ("KAH-len-dih-MAH-dje-oh") festival in May.

FOOD AND THE ARTS

Italy is a gastronomic paradise in summer, with a string of food festivals. Some of these festivals celebrate ripening grapes; others celebrate eating truffles, making olive oil, or harvesting artichokes. Each town has its own specialty, such as strawberries in Nemi, mushrooms in Santa Fiora in Tuscany, calamari in Porto San Giorgio, tomatoes in Angri in Campania, roast pork in Ariccia, and wine in Montefiascone.

Some Italian festivals focus on the arts: opera, theater, film, poetry, or dance. Often, guest performers are invited, even to arts festivals in small towns such as Palermo in Sicily, which hosts a famous puppet festival each year in November.

Italy's most famous arts festival is the Festival of Two Worlds in the Umbrian town of Spoleto. For three weeks in late June to early July, international dancers, musicians, and actors grace Spoleto's stages and streets. Cultural icons such as Al Pacino, Yo-Yo Ma, Mikhail Baryshnikov, and the late Ezra Pound have appeared at the festival.

THE IMPORTANCE OF FESTIVALS

Festivals unite Italians in a common purpose, reacquaint them with the past, and give them a sense of identity in the community. Before a feast day, the people of a town work together regardless of status to hang colored lanterns in the *piazza*, string tiny white lights on churches and monuments, plan fireworks displays, and set up long tables in the town square to hold food for the feast. Families gather to make costumes and cook special meals. Workers take time off from work and soldiers from the army to take part in the festivities.

Before Corpus Christi every June, thousands in the medieval Umbrian town of Spello "paint" enormous, subtly colored replicas of such great works of art as Raphael's *Holy Family* and Michelangelo's *Moses* on the main street using flower petals. Some festivals are so elaborate that organizers begin preparing for next year's event as soon as the present year's ends.

To commemorate a chess game played by two noblemen in 1454 for the hand of a girl, the residents of Marostica, a medieval town in Veneto, turn the main *piazza* into a life-size chess board in September every even-numbered year. The players stand on the board as chess pieces: the knights in armor ride horses, the king and queen wear royal robes, and the castles are floats wheeled by hidden drivers who practice their parts for six months before the game.

Carol Field, author of five award-winning books about Italian food, sums up the significance of festivals in *Celebrating Italy*: "… there are [country festivals] that celebrate asparagus, cherries, lemons, strawberries, apricots …; festivals in honor of geese, frogs, ducks, and thrushes. … Festivals reenact the primal rhythms of the birth and death of seasons and crops, … the great release of warmth from the sun and of moisture from water that causes crops to be born. … Festivals are a key to the secrets of the world."

Spello's main street "painted" with flower petals.

Above: **Women in costume at the Carnival in Venice. Plays, masked balls, and fireworks are held in the city's streets and *piazzas*.**

Opposite: **A group of marchers in a *palio* procession.**

CARNIVAL

Carnival, or *carnevale* ("KAHR-neh-VAH-leh"), which means "goodbye to the flesh," has been celebrated in Italy for centuries. Carnival is held during the 10 days leading to Ash Wednesday, the first day of the season of Lent, which is a time of prayer, self-examination, and fasting in anticipation of Good Friday and Easter.

In the Middle Ages, people wore masks and costumes to Carnival balls, where they ate and drank excessively (the masks ensured anonymity and broke any sense of self-consciousness). The Carnival in Venice once lasted six months.

Carnival is still celebrated intensely in a few cities in Italy, especially Venice and Viareggio. For 10 days, thousands gather in the Piazza San Marco, Venice's most famous square, in fair or freezing weather, to listen to music and to dance, dressed in elaborate masks and fancy costumes as knights, princesses, nuns, popes, or *commedia dell'arte* characters. Other masks are based on more abstract motifs.

There are puppet shows, balls, operas, and drama productions. People caught in mock battles in the streets get hit by mounds of shaving cream. At the end of the festivities, a huge bonfire is lit, and an effigy of the King of Carnival is burned, indicating the end of the days of excess and the start of penitence and abstinence.

The Carnival of Viareggio on the Tuscan coast, officially celebrated since the 1870s, is famous for its seafront float parade. The floats, created by skilled artisans and fitted with sophisticated sound systems, are colorful, funny, and often satirical, parodying famous personalities.

PALIO IN SIENA

The *palio* ("PAH-lee-oh"), the biggest event in the Tuscan city of Siena, is a bareback horse race that originated in the early 14th century.

Celebrated twice a year, in July and August, the festival begins with a slow, dignified march. The groups of marchers, dressed in medieval costumes of silk, fur, and velvet and bearing colorful flags and banners, represent the 17 districts of the medieval Sienese Republic. The marchers make periodic stops, in front of important buildings along the route. The spectators, who number about 20,000, wave colorful scarves, indicating their allegiance to one of the medieval parishes.

The solemnity of the 90-minute procession contrasts with the frenzy of the horse race that follows. Ten jockeys ride their unsaddled horses around Siena's sumptuous Piazza del Campo. There are virtually no rules in the race, and a rider can do almost anything to win. He can strike another jockey or even give bribes. And he can claim victory even if his horse makes it past the finish line without him!

The winning horse-man team receives a banner with an image of the Virgin Mary, and they get to attend a jubilant feast the night after the race as honored guests.

CHRISTMAS

Italian families get together very often, but their gatherings take on a special meaning during the Christmas and Easter seasons. At Christmas,

the family sets up a small nativity scene in a prominent place in the living room. The nativity display may look more like a place in Italy than the town of Bethlehem where Jesus was born, and the figures in the creche may be dressed like Italians. The figures can be made from paper, clay, or stone, depending on the wealth of the family, and sets are passed from generation to generation.

Outside, the chilly streets of Italy's northern cities come alive in December: shops glitter with tiny white lights; wandering "shepherds" playing bagpipe-like instruments do their rounds; and street vendors sell roasted chestnuts.

For children, Christmas is also the excitement of opening their gifts.

Like North Americans, Italian families put up a Christmas tree in the living room. They also burn a yule log called *ceppo* ("CHAY-poh") each night, and the children traditionally receive gifts on Christmas and on Epiphany. The second round of gifts comes from a kind old fairy called Befana. The presents go to the good children, of course, while those who have been naughty supposedly get coal and ashes.

Christmas brings back family members living away from home. On Christmas Eve, the extended family gathers for a multicourse dinner that often centers on fish, eel being the most important dish. (Fish markets in Italy display tanks of live eel during the Christmas season to entice shoppers.) During the family feast, the children sing carols and receive coins or praise from the older relatives. An ancient game similar to bingo follows the feast, and at midnight everyone attends Mass.

HOLY WEEK

Celebrations during the week leading up to Easter include processions that reenact the life and death of Jesus Christ. In some towns, young men strike their legs (*right*) with pieces of cork studded with broken glass to experience a bit of the pain that Jesus Christ endured on Good Friday.

The Monday after Easter is a national holiday, often spent with the family at a picnic, if the weather permits. All who can make a pilgrimage to some grassy spot spread out a large picnic blanket and lay it with delicious food.

Easter Monday fare includes hardboiled eggs (symbolizing rebirth), sandwiches, pizza, lamb (symbolizing innocence), salads, sweets, wine, and fruit. In Sicily, people eat roasted artichokes, country bread, grilled lamb, and a grain dish. The Sicilian Easter sponge cake has layers of sweetened ricotta and candied fruit. Tiny lamb-shaped candies, chocolate eggs, and dough-covered, doll-shaped hardboiled eggs are other treats.

The whole family regroups on Christmas Day, after having attended another Mass, for another grand dinner. This often starts with a very rich stuffed pasta served in broth, moves on to a still richer stuffed turkey or capon, and ends with traditional sweets that vary according to the region. *Panettone* ("pah-nay-TOH-nay") is a fruit sponge cake familiar to all Italians at Christmas. The typical *panettone* is made with raisins and candied fruit, but each region has its own version. Some versions are coated in chocolate, others in toasted nuts.

Other Christmas treats include *torrone* ("TOH-roh-nay"), or nougat, *struffoli* ("stroo-FOH-lee"), or fried egg pastry coated with honey and colored sugar, and panforte ("pahn-FOR-tay"), gingerbread made with hazelnuts and almonds.

Northern Italians generally enjoy larger feasts than many southern families, whose holiday dinners may consist of only fish dishes. (Some, however, serve nine, 13, or 24 courses.) In the south, the family feast is grander on Christmas Eve than on Christmas Day, while in the north it is the exact opposite.

FOOD

ITALIANS LOVE FOOD and consider good cooking an art. They are intensely proud of their traditional cuisine, which originated over 2,000 years ago. Ancient Etruscan tombs were decorated with domestic scenes that showed cooking utensils such as rolling pins and pasta cutters, and the upper-class citizens of ancient Rome were known to dine in great splendor and excess.

First- and second-century writers such as Decimus Junius Juvenalis, who wrote several satires on many aspects of Roman society, and Gaius Petronius, whose *Satyricon* portrays the newly rich Trimalchio's dinner party, described in their accounts the kinds of food laid on the banquet tables of the wealthiest Romans. The menu included at least three courses—appetizer, main, and desert—and often featured exotic meats such as hare, gazelle, peacock, and even flamingo. Pike liver, sea urchin, oysters, stuffed wild fowl, and tender shoots of leek were some other luxuries for the tastebuds. Bread was served on silver plates.

Other items included seafood such as salmon, shark, lobster, and octopus, poultry such as goose and pheasant, dairy foods such as eggs, milk, and cheese, vegetables such as artichokes, celery, truffles, and radishes, and fruit such as olives, figs, plums, cherries, dates, and grapes. The main dishes were elaborately prepared, using different seasonings such as saffron, mint, vinegar, honey, and mustard.

Italians claim to have taught the rest of Europe to cook, and they are essentially correct. In the 16th century, Catherine de Medici brought Florentine cooks to France after she married King Henry. Today Italian food is popular around the world. Spaghetti and pizza have been in the United States for so long that many there probably think of these as American. Few people know that Italy is also responsible for introducing the world to ice cream, coffee, French fries, and fruit pies.

"At the table, no one grows old."

—*old Italian proverb*

Opposite: **Bread, cheese, meats such as pepperoni and salami, and of course wine make up an Italian picnic.**

119

A greengrocer's stall. Open fresh food markets are popular in Italy.

GROCERY SHOPPING

Fresh ingredients are essential to most Italian cooks. Many homemakers shop daily for the freshest meat, fruit, and vegetables. There is an open market in each village or town, and several in each city. Some of the stalls in these markets have been run by the same family for generations.

In Rome, every neighborhood has a small market where residents can buy fresh seasonal produce. The larger markets are colorful, bustling places. Some stalls sell fresh fragrant fruit and vegetables such as plump red tomatoes, wild strawberries, and Italian blood-red oranges. Others offer fish direct from the sea such as swordfish, tuna, eel, squid, and octopus. Still others have herbs, dried and fresh beans, wild mushrooms, breads, olive oils, and cheeses. Butchers sell sausages of all sizes as well as cuts of pork, lamb, and veal.

While shopping for ingredients, people can stop at stalls selling prepared foods for a snack: a slice of pizza, a ham or cheese sandwich, or a bowl of hot, homemade soup.

A pizza and sandwich stall in the market, where people stop for a quick snack before getting back to their shopping.

Aside from open markets, Italians also shop for groceries in large supermarkets, or *supermercato*, complete with convenience foods such as dried pasta, sliced bread, and canned and frozen foods.

There are also small stores licensed by the government to sell specialty items: the *panetteria* ("pah-nay-teh-REE-ah") sells bread, rolls, and other freshly baked foods; the butcher shop, or *salumeria* ("sah-loo-meh-REE-ah"), sells delicatessen items such as sausages and cheeses; milk, yogurt, and some cheeses can be purchased at the *latteria* ("laht-tuh-REE-ah"), beef, veal, and poultry at the *macelleria* ("mah-cheh-luh-REE-ah"), fish at the *pescheria* ("pes-keh-REE-ah"), fresh fruit and vegetables at the *fruttivendolo* ("froot-te-VEN-doh-loh"), and canned goods at the convenience store, or *alimentari* ("ah-lee-men-TAH-re"). Shopping in the small stores takes time, but many Italian homemakers prefer to do so for fresher, tastier food and for a chat with the store owners.

Urbanites often buy roast chicken and other prepared dishes at a *rosticceria* ("ro-sti-chay-REE-ah"), or "cookhouse."

REGIONAL SPECIALTIES

Italian cooking is wonderfully diverse and creative. Just as each region of Italy has its own dialect, so too does it have its own special dishes and styles of cooking. In the past, corn and rice formed the base for the northern Italian diet, while southern Italians ate primarily pasta. However, these staples are no longer so strictly defined geographically. Pasta served in the north is generally flat, such as *capelli d'angelo* ("kah-PEH-lih DAHN-jeh-loh") and *linguine* ("lin-GWE-neh"), while that served in the south is tubular, such as *penne* ("PEH-neh") and macaroni. Northern Italians tend to cook with butter, while southerners use olive oil.

An old shop in Bologna sells the various sausages and *prosciutto* the city is famous for.

Italian cooks prefer to use ingredients grown locally, and each region is famous for its specialties, cooked using traditional methods. The best egg pasta, Parmesan cheese, and *prosciutto* ("proh-SHOO-toh"), or thinly sliced cured ham, come from Emilia-Romagna; the freshest fish dishes and flakiest pastries from Sicily; and the tastiest rice dishes from Veneto.

Many of the major cities are known for a particular dish: Rome for the choicest roast lamb, Milan for the richest *minestrone* ("me-nes-TROH-ne") soup, Genoa for the most authentic *gnocchi* ("NYOK-ki") dumplings and *pesto* ("PES-toh") sauce, Naples for its pizza, Florence for its beef dishes, and Bologna for its lasagne and *mortadella* ("mor-tah-DEL-lah"), or sausage flecked with bits of peppercorns.

Italians are generally conservative in their food preferences and protective of their culinary traditions.

In 1986 the opening of Italy's first McDonald's restaurant in Rome caused an uproar. The historical significance of the location—the Piazza di Spagna—was an added concern. Food purists protested outside the restaurant, giving away free spaghetti to remind Italians of their culinary heritage.

Today, that McDonald's outlet is one of the world's busiest, and there are more than 200 outlets throughout the country employing thousands of people. But some Italians have not forgiven its intrusion into Rome's historic district. A nonprofit movement calling itself Slow Food (with a snail for its symbol) tries to persuade Italians to preserve the art of dining, of making meals a leisurely and pleasurable experience.

RISOTTO IN THE NORTH   In the northern provinces of Lombardy, Piedmont, and Veneto, a rice dish called *risotto* ("ree-ZOT-toh") replaces pasta at lunch and dinner. To make basic traditional *risotto*, rice from the Po Valley is boiled in a little homemade broth. As the rice absorbs the liquid, the cook adds a ladleful of broth and stirs the mixture. This is repeated a few times for about 20 minutes until the rice is plump. Then the cook adds butter, freshly grated Parmesan cheese, and saffron.

Sometimes other ingredients such as chicken, shrimp, sausage, ham, liver, herbs, vegetables, beans, and mushrooms are added. The regional dish of Venice is *risotto* made with peas. Very special *risotto* dishes are made with white truffles or black squid ink.

Just as perfect pasta is served *al dente* ("ahl DEN-teh"), which means "at the teeth," perfect *risotto* must be served *all'onda* ("ahl OHN-dah"), which means "rippling" or "in waves."

Italian cooking has been influenced by other cuisines. The cooking in Sicily is said to be Greek in origin, and that of Sardinia Phoenician. The northeastern cuisines show Austrian, Hungarian, and Slovenian influences. And Italian pasta is claimed by some to have been brought from China by Marco Polo, the Venetian explorer.

The Arabs brought dried pasta to Italy in the 13th century, and pasta has been part of the Italian's daily diet since the 15th century.

PASTA IN THE SOUTH Pasta forms part of the daily diet of southern Italians and many northerners as well. Pasta was commonly eaten with honey and sugar; tomato sauce was not added until the 17th and 18th centuries. Pasta was originally eaten using the fingers. One would simply pick up a few strands or pieces, tilt the head back, and gently lower the pasta into the mouth. Pasta was traditionally handmade by the mother of the household, who passed her techniques down to her daughters.

Amazingly enough, there are more than 500 different varieties of pasta eaten in Italy today, all made with the simple ingredients of flour, water, and sometimes eggs. Traditionally, the poorer southern Italians made pasta with just flour and water; only the northerners could afford eggs.

The names and shapes of some types of pasta reflect Italians' creativity and sense of humor: spaghetti means "little strings," the thinner *capelli d'angelo* is "angels' hair," the flatter and wider *linguine* translates as "little tongues," and the ridged, tubular *sedani* ("SAY-dah-ne") are "celery stalks." There are other kinds of pasta called "little mustaches," "little ears," "bow-tie," "greedy priests," "priest stranglers," and "car-door handles."

The shape, length, and thickness of each type of pasta relate directly to how it is cooked and how much sauce it can absorb. Thin noodles are best served with a light dressing, while thicker ones go well with a heavier cream or tomato sauce. Little shells and elbow macaroni are perfect for soups, while larger shells and macaronis such as *rigatoni* ("re-gah-TOH-ne") are baked stuffed with cheese.

PIZZA FROM NAPLES Pizza's true home is Naples, where pizza chefs apprentice for two to three years before earning their qualifications. Classic Neapolitan pizzas include the cheeseless *pizza marinara* ("mah-re-NAH-rah"), using oregano, tomato sauce, and large hunks of garlic, and *pizza Margherita,* made with tomato sauce, local cheeses, and basil. (The latter is named for Queen Margherita of the House of Savoy, who praised it while visiting Naples in 1889.) Both pizzas are drizzled with olive oil before being baked for only two minutes in a large wood-burning oven shaped like an igloo.

Other less traditional Neapolitan pizzas include the *quattro stagioni* ("KWA-troh stah-JOE-neh"), made with mozzarella cheese and separate sections of mushrooms, seafood, anchovies, and capers, and *pizza alla pescatora* ("pes-kah-TOH-rah"), made with a combination of seafood such as clams, squid, and shrimp. Neapolitans in a hurry buy fried pizza snacks, cooked in hot oil, from street vendors.

Participants in a Carnival parade take time out for pizza.

A glass of red wine complements a plate of Tuscan-style pasta.

ITALIAN WINES

Italy's wine history dates from classical times when the ancient Cretans called the Italian regions Enotria, the land of wine. Until recently, only the famous *Chianti* ("ke-AHN-te"), a red wine from the Tuscany region, was well-known outside Italy. Yet the vast Italian vineyards produce a fine variety of wines and make Italy the world's largest wine producer.

To guarantee the quality of its wines, the Italian authorities set strict regulations to control the production and pressing of the grapes and the ageing and bottling of the wines. Bottles with a consistent quality of wine have DOC (Controlled Denomination of Origin) labels; only these wines are fit for export.

Italian wines have found their diversity in the country's numerous regional vineyards. The hilly areas of Tuscany, Friuli-Venezia Giulia, and Lazio are famous for their high-quality red wines, as are the plains of

Lombardy and Emilia-Romagna. Liguria, Trentino-Alto Adige, and Veneto produce world-famous white wines. Italy's *Spumante* ("spoo-MAHN-teh"), a soft, mellow, sparkling white wine, is becoming well-known and fashionable in the Italian home market. Like champagne, this wine is usually drunk on special occasions.

MEALS AND MEALTIMES

Italians eat three meals a day: a simple breakfast at about 8 A.M., a long lunch at 1 or 2 P.M., and a late dinner at about 8 or 9 P.M. Breakfast usually consists of coffee and bread or a roll. On the way to work, many city dwellers grab a quick breakfast at a café. They usually have a small cup of strong coffee and a sweet crescent roll.

Lunch, or *pranzo* ("PRAHN-zoh"), is the most important meal of the day. If possible, parents and children come home to have a leisurely multicourse meal together.

As a rule, each course is served separately, and the plates are cleared before the next course. First may be an appetizer, or *antipasto* ("AHN-te-PAHS-toh"), literally meaning "pre-food." This often consists of a cold seafood salad, thin salami or ham slices served with melon, or artichoke hearts or mushrooms served with oil and vinegar. Often soup is served instead of *antipasto*.

The next course is a pasta or rice dish, followed by a main course of poultry, meat, or fish. Vegetables, salad, or cheese accompany the main courses, and bread is served throughout the meal. Fruit or a light sweet dessert is followed by coffee.

The evening meal is often similar to lunch and may be even more elaborate if there are visitors. Wine and mineral water are drunk at both lunch and dinner.

Wine stories abound in the regions of Italy. In one such story, a wine-loving German bishop traveling to Rome sent his steward ahead to scout for the inns with the best wine. The man was supposed to chalk "Est," meaning "It is," on the door of the inns with good wine. At Montefiascone, the bishop finally found his man, dead in front of a door marked "Est! Est!! Est!!!" And this, today, is the name of Lazio's best known wine.

A little boy has a hard time deciding which flavor to choose at a *gelateria*.

GELATO

Italian ice cream is called *gelato* ("jeh-LAH-toh"), meaning "frozen." Big cities have *gelateria* ("jeh-lah-teh-REE-ah"), or ice-cream bars. *Gelato* may be served in thick slices cut from a *cassata* ("kah-SAH-tah"), a mound of various ice creams with chopped candied fruit and nuts. Flavors of *gelato* include *cioccolato* ("choh-ko-LAH-to"), *stracciatella* ("strah-chah-TEL-ah"), or chocolate chip, *nocciola* ("noh-CHOH-lah"), or hazelnut, *caffè* ("kah-FEH"), and *malaga* ("mah-LAH-gah"), or rum and raisin. Sherbet is made with peaches, strawberries, raspberries, melon, apples, kiwi, or bananas. Some shops serve unusual flavors such as champagne or avocado sherbet or rice or celery *gelato*.

Italian ice cream is said to be lighter and tastier than North American ice cream. Good *gelateria* use only fresh ingredients, fresh fruit, or—for their coffee ice cream—freshly brewed *espresso* ("es-PRES-so"), in addition to the essential cream, sugar, and egg yolks. Tubs of fresh ice cream are displayed topped with pieces of fresh fruit and signs reading "homemade."

When it comes to preparing and eating exotic *gelato,* Italians are much more experimental than they are in trying a new pasta sauce. They do not hesitate to mix unlikely flavors in the same cup, and they are often eager to try the newest flavors or combinations at their favorite *gelateria.*

COFFEE

Italian coffee is always made from freshly ground beans, usually very strong. But there are many ways Italians like their coffee:

Espresso senza schiuma ("SEHN-zah SHYOO-mah") is a small cup of strong coffee without foam on top, while *espresso con molta schiuma* ("kon MOL-tah SHYOO-mah") is strong coffee with a lot of foam.

Espresso lungo, a "long" coffee, is a slightly larger cup of coffee that takes longer to drink, while *espresso al volo* ("ahl VOH-loh"), coffee "in flight," is a regular *espresso* served up quickly for someone in a hurry.

Espresso macchiato ("mah-CHEEAH-toh"), "spotted" coffee, has a drop of milk in it, while *espresso corretto* ("koh-REH-toh") has a bit of alcohol added. *Espresso al vetro* ("ahl VEH-tro") is served in a glass rather than a cup. (Some Italians think it tastes better this way.)

Cappuccino ("kah-pu-CHEE-no") is coffee with hot, foamy milk. *Cappuccino* is served on ice, warm, or very hot. It may be "light," with a good amount of milk, or "dark," with just a little milk.

Caffè latte ("LAH-teh") is coffee with an equal proportion of milk.

Some Italians enjoy sitting at a café table for hours, while others prefer to drink their coffee quickly and while standing. In Italy, you pay about half the price if you stand and drink your cup rather than slowly sipping it at a table. Many Italians simply stand around the coffee bar, chatting with other customers while balancing their cup of coffee in one hand and a sweet roll in the other.

The first Westerners to import coffee were the Venetians in 1615. The first Italian cookbook was written in 1474 by Bartolomeo Sicci.

PIZZA MARINARA

1 cup lukewarm water
2¼ teaspoons active yeast
1 teaspoon sugar
1 teaspoon salt
1 tablespoon extra-virgin olive oil
3 cups unbleached or bread flour
1 teaspoon corn meal

Additional olive oil
Sliced fresh tomatoes or prepared pasta sauce
Sprinkle of dried or fresh oregano
Shredded mozzarella cheese
Fresh basil leaves or sliced mushrooms or diced
bell peppers or sliced olives (optional)

Pour the water into a large mixing bowl, and sprinkle the yeast on top. Leave for five minutes. Then stir and add the sugar and salt and 1 tablespoon of oil, beating well. Stir in half the flour, and beat until smooth. Add as much of the rest of the flour as necessary to make the dough just firm enough to manage. Knead the dough in the bowl or on a floured board for about five minutes, until smooth. Roll the dough into a ball and flatten. Sprinkle the corn meal over a pizza pan. Pull and stretch the dough gently to fill the pan, and press the edges up to make a slight rim. Leave for 15 minutes to rise. Lightly brush the dough with olive oil. Spread the tomato slices or pasta sauce over the dough and sprinkle with oregano. Spread the mozzarella cheese over the dough. Top with fresh basil leaves, sliced mushrooms, diced bell peppers, sliced olives, or other topping. Bake in preheated oven at 425°F (218°C) for 25 to 30 minutes, depending on the amount of topping.

CANNOLI SICILIANI

This recipe makes 14 to 18 servings.

1½ cups ricotta cheese
3 tablespoons sugar
1½ teaspoons cinnamon
1½ cups (4–5 bars) coarsely chopped milk chocolate
¼ cup coarsely chopped pistachio nuts
14 to 18 cannoli shells
Confectioner's sugar

Beat the cheese in a bowl for about a minute. Add the sugar and beat for about 5 minutes until very light and creamy. Fold in the cinnamon and chopped chocolate and nuts. Place the cheese mixture in a disposable plastic pastry bag and refrigerate for at least 2 hours before piping into shells. Use a long teaspoon to fill the shells with the mixture. Fill the shells just before serving so that they do not become soggy. Arrange the filled shells on a tray, and sprinkle confectioners' sugar on top. Serve immediately.

A　　　**B**　　　**C**　　　**D**

SWITZERLAND

AUSTRIA

HUNGARY

Matterhorn
(14,692 ft)

TRENTINO-
ALTO ADIGE

FRIULI
VENEZIA
GIULIA

SLOVENIA

N

Monte Bianco
(15,577 ft)

Trento

Monte
Marmolada
(10,965 ft)

Udine

CROATIA

1

VALLE
D'AOSTA

Lake
Como

Lake
Garda

VENETO

Trieste

FRANCE

Como

Brescia

Verona

Venice

Turin

Milan

Padua

PIEDMONT

Po

LOMBARDY

Po

BOSNIA &
HERZEGOVINA

LIGURIA

EMILIA-ROMAGNA

MONACO

Genoa

Bologna

La
Spezia

SAN
MARINO

YUGOSLAVIA

Viareggio

L I G U R I A N

Pisa
Arno

Florence

Ancona

2

S E A

TUSCANY

MARCHE

Siena

Perugia

Assisi
Spello

Porto San
Giorgio

Santa
Fiora

UMBRIA

Elba

Spoleto

Monte Corno
(9,554 ft)

Corsica
(FRANCE)

Montefiascone

Pescara

ABRUZZI

Tiber

ROME

Strait of Bonifacio

Ariccia

MOLISE

LAZIO

3

Foggia

Bari

CAMPANIA

Naples

APULIA

Pompeii

Brindisi

Ischia

BASILICATA

Taranto

SARDINIA

Gulf of
Taranto

T Y R R H E N I A N

CALABRIA

Cagliari

S E A

I O N I A N

4

M

SEA

E

D

Palermo

Messina

Reggio di
Calabria

I

Madonie
Mountains

Monte Etna
(10,902 ft)

● Capital city

● Major town

▲ Mountain peak

T

E

SICILY

Feet　　Meters

R

Catania

16,500　5,000

R

Strait of Sicily

Strait of Messina

9,900　3,000

A

Syracuse

6,600　2,000

ALGERIA

N

3,300　1,000

E

1,650　500

5

A

N

S E A

660　200

TUNISIA

MALTA

0　0

MAP OF ITALY

ECONOMIC ITALY

Agriculture

- Fruit
- Vegetables
- Olives
- Wheat
- Sheep
- Wine
- Tobacco

Services

- Airport
- Port
- Tourism

Natural Resources

- Fish

Manufacturing

- Crafts
- Textiles
- Silk
- Vehicles

ABOUT THE ECONOMY

GDP
$1.273 trillion (2000)
Per capita: $22,100

GDP SECTORS
Agriculture 2.5 percent, industry 30.4 percent, services 67.1 percent

LAND USE
Arable land 31 percent, permanent pastures 15 percent, permanent crops 10 percent, forests and woodland 23 percent, other 21 percent

AGRICULTURAL PRODUCTS
Fruit (especially grapes), potatoes, sugar beets, soybeans, grain, olives, beef, dairy products, fish

INDUSTRIAL PRODUCTS
Food products, textiles and clothing, footwear, ceramics, motor vehicles, machinery, iron and steel, chemicals

CURRENCY
The euro (EUR) replaced the Italian lire (ITL) in 2002 at a fixed rate of 1,936.27 lires per euro.
1 euro = 100 cents
USD 1 = EUR 1.03 (August 2002)
Notes: 5, 10, 20, 50, 100, 200, 500 euros
Coins: 1, 2, 5, 10, 20, 50 cents; 1, 2 euros

LABOR FORCE
23.4 million (2000)

LABOR DISTRIBUTION
Agriculture 5.5 percent, industry 32.6 percent, services 61.9 percent

UNEMPLOYMENT RATE
10.4 percent (2000)

INFLATION RATE
2.5 percent (2000)

MAJOR TRADE PARTNERS
Germany, France, the Netherlands, Spain, the United States

TOTAL EXPORTS
$241.1 billion (2000)

TOTAL IMPORTS
$231.4 billion (2000)

PORTS AND HARBORS
Bari, Brindisi, Genoa, La Spezia, Naples, Palermo, Trieste, Venice

AIRPORTS
135 total; 97 with paved runways (2000)

COMMUNICATIONS MEDIA
Telephone: 25 million operating main lines; 20.5 million mobile cellular phones (2000)
Television: 41 sets per 100 inhabitants (1999)
Internet: 11.6 million users (2000)

135

CULTURAL ITALY

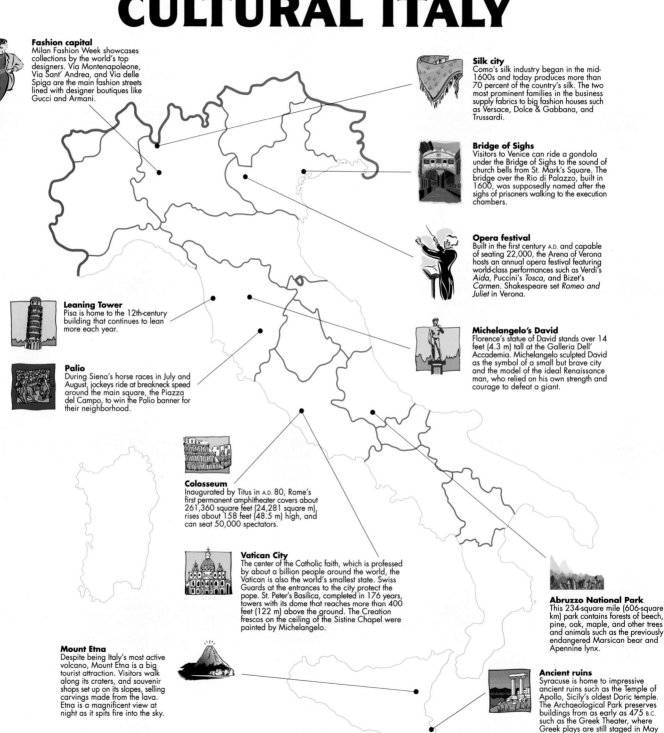

Fashion capital
Milan Fashion Week showcases collections by the world's top designers. Via Montenapoleone, Via Sant' Andrea, and Via delle Spiga are the main fashion streets lined with designer boutiques like Gucci and Armani.

Silk city
Como's silk industry began in the mid-1600s and today produces more than 70 percent of the country's silk. The two most prominent families in the business supply fabrics to big fashion houses such as Versace, Dolce & Gabbana, and Trussardi.

Bridge of Sighs
Visitors to Venice can ride a gondola under the Bridge of Sighs to the sound of church bells from St. Mark's Square. The bridge over the Rio di Palazzo, built in 1600, was supposedly named after the sighs of prisoners walking to the execution chambers.

Opera festival
Built in the first century A.D. and capable of seating 22,000, the Arena of Verona hosts an annual opera festival featuring world-class performances such as Verdi's *Aida*, Puccini's *Tosca*, and Bizet's *Carmen*. Shakespeare set *Romeo and Juliet* in Verona.

Leaning Tower
Pisa is home to the 12th-century building that continues to lean more each year.

Michelangelo's David
Florence's statue of David stands over 14 feet (4.3 m) tall at the Galleria Dell' Accademia. Michelangelo sculpted David as the symbol of a small but brave city and the model of the ideal Renaissance man, who relied on his own strength and courage to defeat a giant.

Palio
During Siena's horse races in July and August, jockeys ride at breakneck speed around the main square, the Piazza del Campo, to win the Palio banner for their neighborhood.

Colosseum
Inaugurated by Titus in A.D. 80, Rome's first permanent amphitheater covers about 261,360 square feet (24,281 square m), rises about 158 feet (48.5 m) high, and can seat 50,000 spectators.

Vatican City
The center of the Catholic faith, which is professed by about a billion people around the world, the Vatican is also the world's smallest state. Swiss Guards at the entrances to the city protect the pope. St. Peter's Basilica, completed in 176 years, towers with its dome that reaches more than 400 feet (122 m) above the ground. The Creation frescos on the ceiling of the Sistine Chapel were painted by Michelangelo.

Abruzzo National Park
This 234-square mile (606-square km) park contains forests of beech, pine, oak, maple, and other trees and animals such as the previously endangered Marsican bear and Apennine lynx.

Mount Etna
Despite being Italy's most active volcano, Mount Etna is a big tourist attraction. Visitors walk along its craters, and souvenir shops set up on its slopes, selling carvings made from the lava. Etna is a magnificent view at night as it spits fire into the sky.

Ancient ruins
Syracuse is home to impressive ancient ruins such as the Temple of Apollo, Sicily's oldest Doric temple. The Archaeological Park preserves buildings from as early as 475 B.C. such as the Greek Theater, where Greek plays are still staged in May and June.

ABOUT THE CULTURE

OFFICIAL NAME
Italian Republic

NATIONAL FLAG
Three equal vertical bands: green, white, and red. Inspired by the French flag that Napoleon brought to Italy in 1797.

NATIONAL ANTHEM
Fratelli d'Italia (Brothers of Italy). Adopted in 1946. Words written by Goffredo Mameli; music composed by Michele Novaro.

CAPITAL
Rome

OTHER MAJOR CITIES
Bologna, Florence, Genoa, Milan, Naples, Palermo, Turin, Venice

ADMINISTRATIVE DIVISIONS
Abruzzi, Apulia, Basilicata, Calabria, Campania, Emilia-Romagna, Friuli-Venezia Giulia, Lazio, Liguria, Lombardy, Marche, Molise, Piedmont, Sardinia, Sicily, Tuscany, Trentino-Alto Adige, Umbria, Valle d'Aosta, Veneto

POPULATION
57,679,825 (2001 est.)

LIFE EXPECTANCY
79.14 years (2001)

ETHNIC MAJORITY
Italian

RELIGIOUS GROUPS
Roman Catholic majority, established Protestant and Jewish communities, growing Muslim immigrant community

LANGUAGES
Italian (official), German (parts of Trentino-Alto Adige), French (Valle d'Aosta), Slovene (Trieste)

PUBLIC HOLIDAYS
New Year's Day (January 1); Epiphany (January 6); Easter Monday (March/April); Independence Day (March 17); Liberation Day (April 25); Labor Day (May 1); Republic Day (June 2); Feast of the Assumption (August 15); All Saints' Day (November 1); Feast of the Immaculate Conception (December 8); Christmas Day (December 2); Saint Stephen's Day (December 26)

FAMOUS RENAISSANCE ARTISTS
Giovanni Bellini, Sandro Botticelli, Donato Bramante, Filippo Brunelleschi, Michelangelo Buonarotti, Tommaso Cassai, Leonardo da Vinci, Donatello, Andrea Palladio, Raffaello Sanzio

OTHER LEADERS IN THE ARTS
Giacomo Puccini, Giuseppe Verdi, Luciano Pavarotti (opera); Amedeo Modigliani (painting); Dante Alighieri, Umberto Eco, Luigi Pirandello (literature)

TIME LINE

IN ITALY	IN THE WORLD
2,000–800 B.C. Latins and Italics arrive; Etruscans in 1200 B.C.; Greeks and Phoenicians in 800 B.C.	**810 B.C.** Phoenicians establish Carthage.
509 B.C. The first Roman republic is established.	
272 B.C. Rome conquers Italy.	**146 B.C.** Romans destroy Carthage in the Punic Wars.
116–17 B.C. The Roman empire reaches its greatest extent, under Emperor Trajan (98–17).	
	A.D. 600 Height of Mayan civilization
A.D. 800 The Holy Roman empire is established.	
	1000 The Chinese perfect gunpowder and begin to use it in warfare.
1434 The Santa Maria del Fiore is completed with Filippo Brunelleschi's famous dome.	
1478–80 War between Florence, Venice, and Milan, and the Papacy, Siena, and Naples	
1495–97 Leonardo da Vinci paints *The Last Supper*.	
1508–12 Michelangelo paints the ceiling of the Sistine Chapel.	**1530** Beginning of trans-Atlantic slave trade organized by the Portuguese in Africa.
	1558–1603 Reign of Elizabeth I of England
	1620 Pilgrim Fathers sail the *Mayflower* to America.
1755 Genoa sells Corsica to France.	**1776** U.S. Declaration of Independence
	1789–1799 The French Revolution
1796–97 Napoleon's army invades Italy.	

IN ITALY	IN THE WORLD
1831	
Birth of the Risorgimento movement	
1861	**1861**
The United Kingdom of Italy is proclaimed.	The U.S. Civil War begins.
	1869
1870	The Suez Canal is opened.
Rome becomes the capital.	
	1914
1915	World War I begins.
Italy enters World War I.	
1925	
Mussolini becomes dictator.	**1939**
1940	World War II begins.
Italy enters World War II on Germany's side.	
1944	
Allied forces seize Rome.	**1945**
	The United States drops atomic bombs on Hiroshima and Nagasaki.
1949	**1949**
Italy joins NATO.	The North Atlantic Treaty Organization (NATO) is formed.
1957	**1957**
Italy joins the European Community (EC).	The Russians launch Sputnik.
	1966–1969
	The Chinese Cultural Revolution
	1986
	Nuclear power disaster at Chernobyl in Ukraine
	1991
1994	Break-up of the Soviet Union
Silvio Berlusconi is investigated for corruption and resigns.	**1997**
1999	Hong Kong is returned to China.
Azeglio Ciampi is sworn in as president.	
2001	**2001**
Berlusconi becomes prime minister.	World population surpasses 6 billion.
2002	
The euro replaces the lire.	

GLOSSARY

a fracetto ("ah frah-CHEH-toh")
The way two men or women walk arm-in-arm, showing friendship

antipasto ("AHN-te-PAHS-toh")
An appetizer of cold dishes served before the main course at lunch or dinner

bocce ("BOH-chay")
A relaxing type of lawn bowling

calcio ("KAHL-choh")
Soccer, the national sport

carnevale ("kahr-neh-VAH-leh")
Literally "goodbye to the flesh," this great festival is celebrated for 10 days prior to Ash Wednesday, the beginning of Lent.

ciao ("CHAOW")
An informal greeting that can mean either hello or goodbye

commedia dell'arte ("kom-MAY-diah del-LAHR-teh")
A style of popular theater developed during the Renaissance

gelato ("jeh-LAH-toh")
A frozen dessert, such as ice cream and sherbet

Giro d'Italia
Italy's biggest cycling marathon attracts cyclists from other countries as well and is celebrated by crowds and covered by the mass media.

la bella figura ("lah BEL-lah fe-GOO-rah")
Literally "beautiful figure," this term refers to refined and cultured behavior.

Mezzogiorno ("med-zoh-JOR-noh")
"Land of the Midday Sun," indicates the southern regions of Italy

panettone ("pah-nay-TOH-nay")
A Christmas sponge cake, usually with raisins and candied fruit

passeggiata ("pah-say-JAH-tah")
An evening stroll in the neighborhood to socialize

piazza ("pe-AHT-zah")
The town square

Renaissance
The era of artistic and intellectual rebirth that lifted Europe out of the Middle Ages

Risorgimento ("ree-sohr-gee-MEN-toh")
Meaning "Resurgence," a 19th-century movement for Italian unification

risotto ("re-ZOT-toh")
Rice boiled in broth, with butter and Parmesan cheese added; commonly eaten in northern Italy.

scirocco ("SHE-roh-koh")
A hot, dry wind that blows across Sicily and the southern Italian provinces in summer, it is laden with very fine red sand from the Sahara Desert in northern Africa.

FURTHER INFORMATION

BOOKS

Alighieri, Dante, and Allen Mandlebaum (translator). *The Divine Comedy: Inferno, Purgatorio, Paradiso*. New York: Knopf, 1995.

Caselli, Giovanni. *In Search of Pompeii: Uncovering a Buried Roman City*. New York: Peter Bedrick Books, 1999.

De Vacchi, Pierluigi, and Gianluigi Colalucci (contributor). *Michelangelo: The Vatican Frescoes*. New York: Abbeville Press, 1997.

Lorenza de' Medici, et. al. *Italy Today the Beautiful Cookbook: Contemporary recipes reflecting simple, fresh Italian cooking*. New York: HarperCollins, 1997.

MacDonald, Hamish. *Mussolini and Italian Fascism*. Pathfinder History Series. Cheltenham, United Kingdom: Stanley Thornes, 1999.

Petronius, and Walsh, P. G. (translator). *The Satyricon*. World's Classics. New York: Oxford University Press, 1999.

Pietro C. Marani. *Leonardo da Vinci: The Complete Paintings*. New York: Harry N. Abrams, Inc., 2000.

Pope John Paul II and John Vitek (editor). *My Dear Young Friends: Pope John Paul II Speaks to Youth on Life, Love, and Courage*. Minnesota: St. Mary's Press, 2002.

WEBSITES

Central Intelligence Agency World Factbook (select "Italy" from the country list). www.cia.gov/cia/publications/factbook

Embassy of Italy in the United States. www.italyemb.org

Italian Ministry of Foreign Affairs. www.esteri.it/eng/index.htm

Italian National Agency for Tourism (ENIT). www.enit.it/default.asp?Lang=UK

Italian Soccer Federation (FIGC). www.figc.it/versione_inglese/default.htm

Lonely Planet World Guide: Destination Italy. www.lonelyplanet.com/destinations/europe/italy

National Institute of Statistics. www.istat.it/English/index.htm

The Roman Empire. www.roman-empire.net

MUSIC

The Most Famous Opera Arias. Various artists. Capitol, 1994.

The Voice of Italy. Various artists. Universal, 2002.

VIDEOS

Discovering Italy. Video Visits Travel Collection. Questar, Inc., 2001.

The Roman Empire in the First Century. PBS Home Video, 2001.

BIBLIOGRAPHY

Birnbaum, Stephen, and Alexandra M. Birnbaum. *Birnbaums Italy 1991*. Boston: Houghton Mifflin Company, 1990.

Camporesi, Piero. *The Magic Harvest: Food, Folklore, and Society*. Cambridge, United Kingdom: Polity Press, 1993.

Dinan, Desmond (editor). *Encyclopedia of the European Union*. Boulder, Colorado: Lynne Rienner Publishers, 2000.

Field, Carol. *Celebrating Italy*. New York: William Morrow and Company, 1990.

Grossman, Ronald. *The Italians in America*. Minneapolis: Lerner, 1990.

Hearder, Harry. *Italy: A Short Story*. New York: Cambridge University Press, 1990.

Murray, William. *The Last Italian: Portrait of a People*. New York: Prentice Hall, 1991.

Pescosolido, Carl. *The Proud Italians: Our Great Civilizers*. Washington, D.C.: The National Italian American Foundation, 1995.

Turner, Barry (editor). *The Statesman's Yearbook 2002: The Politics, Cultures, and Economies of the World*. New York: Palgrave Macmillan, 2001.

Europa World Yearbook 2000.

Windows on Italy. www.mi.cnr.it/WOI/woiindex.html

Food and Agriculture Organization of the United Nations. www.fao.org

United Nations Environmental Program. www.unep.net

INDEX